It is not surprising that stress is a well-known concept in nursing. Nurses, therefore, need sources of continuing strength and refreshment, and of spiritual health and growth, if they are to continue to function fully as effective nurses.

Pat M. Ashworth
A History of Nurses Christian Fellowship International: The First 50 years

A word aptly spoken is like apples of gold in settings of silver. Proverbs 25:11 describes Carrie Dameron's new book CARES perfectly. Just like she does in the regular *Journal of Christian Nursing*, "Christian Nursing 101" column she writes, Carrie weaves Scripture and nursing together throughout these 52 reflections. Her practical application of God's Word to our sacred work and calling in nursing presents a beautiful display of gold and silver.

Kathy Schoonover-Shoffner, Editor
Journal of Christian Nursing

NCFI CARES is like a tonic to the Christian nurse which keeps her/him on her toes and helps her meet the total needs of her client. CARES is also like a manual that guides the nurse on when, how, where, and what to do when faced with difficulty in the process of caring.

Thomas Ibe
Federal Neuro-Psychiatric Hospital,
Calabar. CRS
FCN Nigeria

NCFI CARES has been a regular resource that we have published on social media, and it has greatly encouraged many of our members in the UK and across Europe. Christian nurses in this part of the world often feel isolated from one another and under pressure to conform to a secular health system - NCFI CARES is a regular encouragement and reminder to them of who we really serve in our careers and how to nurse in a Christlike, God-honouring way.

Steve Fouch
Chair, NCFI European Committee
CMF Head of Nursing Ministries

No doubt this book is a tremendous gift from God to us, a compilation of biblical reflections made by Carrie, which will help us to become intimate with God, get closer, and learn to listen. By searching the Scriptures from the essence of nursing practice, we can care the way God cares for us, with "compassion and love."

Alicia Yánez Molina
ACEMACH Chile
Chair, NCFI Latin America Region

CARES

Reflections for Nurses

(English only edition)

Carrie M. Dameron

a nurses4him.org publication

nurses4him.org

passion, purpose, prayer

nurses4|im.org

passion, purpose, prayer

nurses4him.org publication

Greetings from the NCFI President

With a mission to equip Christian nurses to live out their faith in their professional practice, NCFI is pleased to bring you CARES, a devotional book for nurses. The timeless truth of Scripture, as it relates to the nursing profession, and to you as a nurse, will encourage your heart and uplift your soul. Nursing is both a scientific discipline and a sacred calling. May you be drawn closer to our Saviour, the source of all hope, as you read and meditate on His Word. And, may God richly bless you as you serve Him in nursing.

by His grace and for His glory.
Barbara White
NCFI President

Contents

Preface 1

Acknowledgements 2

Introduction 3

Oil for Our Lamps 4

FaitHope 6

Just a Sprinkle 8

A Blanket of Grace 10

One More Tool 12

"Whom Should I Send?" 14

Agapē! 16

Dear Nurse: 18

Peter's Wisdom 20

Global Fellowship 22

The Wise Nurse 24

No Nurses in Heaven! 26

"Come quickly, Lord" 28

Dementia for Today 30

Storehouse of Bread 32

Drops of Kindness 34

Sealed, Secured, and Sanctified 36

A Sabbath Rest 38

A Noun or a Verb? 40

P Purpose & Plan 42

E Energy (Koach) 44

R Resources 46

S Song of the Suffering 48

E Equipped Abundantly 50

V Victory Promised 52

E Enthusiasm 54

R Rally Partners 56

A Adversity's Purpose 58

N Navigating Presence 60

C Courage 62

E Eternal Nursing Crown 64

Adoration 66

Shoes for Chicken Little 68

Looking for the One 70

Revolutionary Nursing 72

Job Well Done! 74

Faith to Rest 76

Path to Humility 78

Spiritual Nutrition 80

A Banner of Thankfulness 82

Critical Reminders 84

Unspoken Prayers 86

Secured in Faithfulness 88

24/7 Protection 90

Choose Joy 92

NG 94

But, Lord!? 96

Who Am I? 98

Seed of Influence 100

In the Trenches 104

Missteps for Opportunity 106

References 108

Resources 109

About the Author 110

Final Note 111

Preface

Welcome to **CARES: Reflections for Nurses!** To truly understand how **CARES** (**C**aring **A**cross **R**egions with **E**ncouraging **S**cripture) has come about is to start with a story involving unexpected blessings. I entered the nursing profession in 1992 as a new Christian and immediately felt ill-equipped to integrate my new faith into nursing (See reflection, "Looking for the One" for my personal experience). I realized I was not alone, for there were many Christian nurses who lacked support in integrating their Christian faith into their professional practice. So, in 2008, I developed an online business, nurses4him.org found at carriedameron.com, to reach out with purpose, passion, and prayer to equip and encourage nurses to merge their faith with their nursing practice (Acts 2:42-44).

In 2010, the story continued through an unpublished Bible study that I sent for review to Kathy Schoonover-Shoffner, editor of the *Journal of Christian Nursing (JCN)*. Kathy and the Lord had more in store than I had imagined through the wider reach of the journal. Kathy inquired if I would write a column using the topics from the Bible study. Amazed by the opportunity, my answer was, "Of course!" The *JCN* column *Christian Nursing 101* debuted in the October/December 2010 issue and continues today.

Then in 2011, through my affiliation with Kathy, I learned about Nurses Christian Fellowship International (NCFI) via an email from Barbara White, NCFI President. I joined an international team of nursing scholars to develop and teach the *Art and Science of Spiritual Care* to Christian nurses worldwide. My heart burst forth, as I came to experience the Lord's work in global nursing. The project was my first international step, literally, for I had yet to secure a passport.

While at the NCFI Congress, in Santiago, Chile, in 2012, I had an informal chat with John White, Barbara's husband. As we chatted, I shared my passion for Christian nurses and he shared the need to connect NCFI nurses beyond the quadrennial congresses. I readily volunteered to email encouraging words to my fellow nurses around the world. So, in January 2013, I emailed the first *NCFI Cares* devotion to national fellowships leaders, nurses, and NCFI staff. Three years later, this bi-monthly devotion is shared via email, Facebook, and on my blog, with a growing recipient list.

In many countries and regions, Internet service is spotty and printed resources are preferred. In 2014, the goal for a published compilation of *NCFI Cares*, available to nurses attending the NCFI Congress in 2016, was developed. Woo-hoo! You hold in your hands that labor of love.

Early on with *NCFI Cares* bimonthly emails, Martha Graciela Fernandez Moyano from Argentina, translated each devotional into Spanish and then forwarded them to nurses in Latin America. Thus, the original **CARES** was published as a bilingual book, with both Spanish and English. At this writing, translation is occuring for a bilingual English and Chinese

Acknowledgements

No book is complete without lots of thanks. This is especially true for an international endeavor resulting in self-publication!

-Hope Graham, NCFI/Canada, was an indispensable reader. Her mature faith and wisdom provided valuable editorial guidance.

-Cathy Walker, Associate Editor for Journal of Christian Nursing, USA, was a reader/editor. Her search for clarity and meaning is indispensable. Any errors are the fault of myself, and not my editorial team.

-Martha Graciela Fernandez Moyano, NCFI/Argentina, provided the Spanish translation, a truly heroic effort. Martha and her team are instrumental in providing *NCFI Cares* to our Spanish-speaking Christian brothers and sisters in Latin America. Any errors in translation, editing or printing are understandable and we both apologize for any confusion this may cause.

-NCFI nurses, national fellowship leaders, and board members who not only endorse **CARES**, but have been a huge support during the writing and publication process. This compilation and the bimonthly devotions *NCFI Cares* is a product of passionate, global Christian nurses who share the love of Christ with one another and the patients they care for—THANKS!

Introduction

Unlike the brief devotions in the bimonthly emails found in *NCFI Cares*, each **CARES** reflection integrates the poignancy of a nurses' devotion, with reflective questions and readings in a brief one-page format. Thus, each reflection includes devotion/discussion with suggested reading, responsorial questions, and prayer. The 52 reflections contained in this publication are a combination of previous devotions sent out as *NCFI Cares*, which have been revised and updated, along with other unpublished Christian nursing topics. Some reflections focus on uplifting your personal faith journey--from your rich faith and walk with Jesus, your nursing care grows and becomes more Christ-like. Other reflections are more directly related to bringing the mercy of God to your patients, families, colleagues, and students.

The reflections in **CARES** are not only for your personal enrichment and faith development. These reflections can guide a mentor/mentee relationship with colleague(s) and/or facilitate prayer and/or encourage fellowship and discussion in a group format. Unique to this edition is the inclusion of a notes page with each reflection to record meditations, doodle insights, and/or pen out prayers and praises. I hope you enjoy the supplement.

As you read and mediate on each reflection, this is my prayer for you:

May our Lord Jesus Christ and God our Father comfort your hearts and give you strength in every good thing you do and say. So that you will be professionally and personally enriched in such a way that the love of Christ spills forth with His grace and love on all entrusted to your care. Amen. (2 Thessalonians 2:16-17)

Oil for Our Lamps

Be dressed for service and keep your lamps burning. (Luke 12:35)

The lamp of nursing is a prominent symbol for our profession. It connects us to our past with Florence Nightingale as "The Lady with the Lamp." For Christians, the oil lamp has further spiritual or theological significance. In the Old Testament, oil was used to consecrate or set-apart people for the Lord's service (Exodus 30:25, 29). In the New Testament, oil was used for healing and for ritual offerings (Luke 10:34; John 12:3).

With these examples in my heart and burning bright in my spirit, I compare myself to an apothecary, mixing a unique, essential oil, by using the topics contained in this reflection book.

I imagine going to my nursing cabinet and finding a bottle of fine essential oil, full of the grace, truth, and love of our Saviour. I stir into the oil drops of prayer, kindness, and joy that build wisdom and humility. Sweetened by the aroma of heaven, a bit of compassion, and a dram each of hope and peace, a rich emollient develops. This results in a thickening agent of perseverance, including faith and courage, blended for both strength and zeal. Clarification removes hate and fear, while solidifying the combined essence of connectedness and leadership. The final refinement is purification through an infusion of the Holy Spirit. The oil is prepared, ready for use.

As nurses, the Lord anoints us for our consecrated work, distinguishing our calling as holy (2 Timothy 1:9; Ephesians 4:4). Now we are ready for the oil to be poured into our individual nursing lamps. Whether we receive a drop, a teaspoon, or a cup, miraculously Jesus accentuates the specific ingredient relevant to each nurses' work. Our exclusive oil will not only light our way, but we can use the healing oil on those entrusted to our care. Look for a time to pour out the oil as an offering before our Saviour—for he is truly the creator and giver of the oil. Finally, remember to keep your lamp full and fresh, ready for use (Matthew 25:4).

Read: Exodus 30:22-30; Matthew 25:1-13

Choose a particular element (hope, peace, etc.) you would like to add to your nursing oil.

Prayer: *Father, consecrate my nursing work with a fresh anointing. Fill my lamp so that I may care for those you have assigned to my care. Amen.*

Notes

FaitHope

All praise to God, the Father of our Lord Jesus Christ. It is by his great mercy
that we have been born again, because God raised Jesus Christ from the dead.
Now we live with great expectation. (1 Peter 1:3)

Whenever we think of hope, in Christianity, we start with Jesus. Our
redemptive Messiah is the source of all hope. An in-depth, biblical search on hope
reveals that Jesus did not specifically teach on hope. Instead, he **is** Hope. As one
Bible scholar[1] puts it, "Jesus is certainty!" Jesus taught and demonstrated why we
should believe in him as the hope for all mankind (John 3:11-16; 1 Peter 1:3). In
addition, he provided an example for us to live out our hope that is secured in
him.

Since Jesus is Hope, our personal faith and hope meld together. For, faith
without hope is meaningless; whereas, hope without faith is fleeting. Romans
8:24-25 teaches, "We were given this hope when we were saved. If we already
have something, we don't need to hope for it. But if we look forward to
something we don't have yet, we must wait patiently and confidently." Bringing
hope to our patients, families, and colleagues begins with fusing our faith and
hope together. Do we truly believe the promises found in God's Word? Or, are
the promises dry religious statements? Are we a hopeful person with our
colleagues and family? If your family and friends were questioned, would they say
you are hopeful and trusting in God the Father to provide? Would they compare
you to the birds of the fields? (Luke 12:22-31) Inspiring hope for our patients
begins with our faith being rooted in the firm foundation of the Alpha and the
Omega, and the promises found in Scripture (Revelation 22:13).

Read: Romans 5:2-5, 8:24-25, 12:12, 15:13

Using the above verses, create a personal definition of hope and faith.

Prayer: *Lord God, consecrate me and root my heart in yours, so that I am always ready to give
an answer for the foundation of my hope. Amen. (1 Peter 3:15)*

Notes

Just a Sprinkle

[Apostle Paul said], "I planted the seed in your hearts, and Apollos watered it, but it was God who made it grow." (1 Corinthians 3:6)

I live in a part of the United States where there is a distinct difference between the "dry" and the "wet" seasons. This has been especially true the past few years. The neighboring hills and fields are a barren tundra of cracked dirt and parched grasses. When the first drops of rain sprinkle across our thirsty landscape, I rejoice. The drops may be just enough to wet the pavement. Yet, with just a little moisture, the hard dirt gives way to small shoots of grass, straining to find the sun. This bit of moisture awakes the grasses in anticipation of nutrients and growth.

I can't help but make the parallel to the human soul or spirit. Just as the drought-ridden dirt and grasses have withering roots, a soul and heart can be barren, without the nourishment of Christ. Whether it is a blade of grass or a dry soul, a drop of moisture can awaken the soul to spring forth in anticipation of renewal.

Sometimes we may think that a non-Christian heart needs a bucket or a river of water to bring growth, not necessarily. All life sprouts anew in response to a sprinkle of water. Imagine the greater miracle when the moisture is the living water of Christ (John 4:14; Revelation 7:17, 22:1). Don't worry about bringing the bucket of salvation. Sprinkle the living water of Christ in your drought-ridden communities, and watch the fruit of the Spirit bloom!

Read: John 4:7-26

How might you bring the living water of Christ to your health care institution?

Prayer: *Jesus, you are living water that provides eternal refreshment. Guide us in sprinkling you around our units, clinics, and organizations. Amen.*

Notes

A Blanket of Grace

From his abundance we have all received one gracious blessing after another.
(John 1:16)

Blanket warmers are common in U.S. acute care hospitals. Similar to kitchen ovens, they have a warm setting and, better yet, they have space to hold many blankets. When patients are cold, nurses can go to the blanket warmer and remove a heated, toasty blanket. I personally like to take two or three to wrap around patients—tucking in their feet, securing one over their shoulders, and sealing in the warmth. It is one of the few comforts patients can't get at home, warm blankets on call.

Grace is comparable to a warm blanket. It is pleasant and comforting, open to everyone. With the soft, fuzziness of kindness and tenderness, grace is a compassionate embrace. Generous in size, grace enfolds the heart, soul, and mind; grace provides the strength to support the weight of the world, while upholding the weak. Our blanket of grace reaches through the dark depths of humanity, even gently nudging the unknowing with the favour of God. Unlike a warm blanket that quickly cools, grace is void of time. Grace is the same yesterday, today, and tomorrow. Grace swaddles our patients, like newborn infants, with the ceaseless sacrifice of lovingkindness.

As nurses, the greatest gift we can give to our patients is the grace of Christ (Romans 3:23-27, 11:32-36). Grace is the mercy of God manifested through our caring touch and tender words. Unlike the warm blankets found in select hospitals, the blanket of grace is freely available to all, in constant and dependable supply.

Read: Titus 3:4-8

Explore tangible ways you can personally bring the merciful grace of Christ to your workplace.

Prayer: *All praise to God, the Father of our Lord Jesus Christ, who is my merciful Father and the source of all my comfort. Amen. (2 Corinthians 1:3)*

Notes

One More Tool

> Are any of you suffering hardships? You should pray. Are any of you
> happy? You should sing praises. (James 5:13)

There are times when our interventions and nursing care are not effective:
we helplessly witness suffering when chemotherapy and radiation fail in saving a
life, when nausea and pain are intractable in our palliative patient, when medical
and surgical interventions are insufficient in the face of severe trauma, when
resources and skill fail to rescue the unborn child and mother, and when
advanced medications and aggressive treatments fall short in the treatment of
patients with substance abuse, depression, or mental illness.

When we face seemingly desperate situations, we can remember there is still
a tool left in our nursing supply box. Sometimes this tool gets buried under
innovative technologies, complex surgical procedures, and evidence-informed
interventions. This tool is just as effective today as it was for Florence
Nightingale, even though it is used less. This is especially true where medical
advancements have paved the way for quicker, more efficient forms of healing.
As nurses, we may forgo honing our skill in using this tool. Instead we pursue
more certifications and degrees. Knowledge has pushed this tool to the bottom of
our patient care treatments. Even though this tool is an integral part of our
Christian faith, it may go unused.

Have you guessed the tool? It is prayer. As a faithful follower of Christ,
prayer is an important intervention. Prayer can heal the sick, save the dying, and
bring hope to the desperate (Acts 4:22, 5:16, 28:8-9). So, let's reach into our tool
box of nursing knowledge, skills, and procedures and bring prayer to the top.
Then we can be reminded to use it first, instead of last.

Read: Matthew 7:7-11; Colossians 1:9-13

Do you feel inhibited to pray with patients? If so, contemplate ways in which you
could take a small step toward being able to pray with or for your patients.

Using Colossians 1:9-13, reflect on attributes that you could silently pray for
patients, families, colleagues, and students.

Prayer: *Lord Jesus, guide me in ways to communicate your love, grace, and peace to those who
need it most. Amen.*

Notes

"Whom Should I Send?"

> Then I heard the Lord asking, "Whom should I send as a messenger to this people? Who will go for us?" I said, "Here I am. Send me." (Isaiah 6:8)

Many times I am asked about the difference between a nurse who is a Christian and a Christian who is a nurse. It is not a unique question. In the church we ask, what is the difference between a Christian and a disciple of Christ? I am not here to say I have the final answer to either question. But, I do have a thought about a defining trait of a Christian nurse—go where Christ calls!

Being obedient to Jesus Christ' command, "Go" (Matthew 28:19) is the difference between a mediocre Christian and a true disciple. Let me explain. As a disciple of Christ, we commit our lives to be lived in obedience to Jesus. We commit to following him in all things. As nurses, this entails going or working where Christ sends us. This may not necessarily be our first choice: whether it is in choosing our specialty, deciding on our educational degree, or selecting to work in the hospital, clinic, or other ministry, our response should be to go. Where Christ sends us may mean being willing to change our career pathway midstream in response to the Lord's directive (Proverbs 16:9; James 4:13-15). Similarly, the response to "Send me!" isn't a one-time only deal. We may wrestle continuously with submitting our lives to our Master, as the one directing each choice, plan, and project as he indicates (John 10:3, 16).

Merging our spiritual gifts and talents, with our nursing knowledge and expertise, we bring mercy, love, and truth to nursing. Raise your hand and say, "Send me!" and see how the Lord perfectly knits his plan, while giving you the desires of your heart (Jeremiah 29:11; Psalm 20:4).

Read: Acts 8:26-40

In Acts 8:26-40, we read the story of Philip sharing the Gospel with the eunuch, then miraculously finding himself in the town of Azotus. Reflect on the heart of Philip and how he willing submitted his life to go wherever God sent him.

How willing are you to being used by God in Christian nursing?

Prayer: *Master, my heart's desire is to serve you with all my talents and nursing knowledge. Open my ears and direct my vision to how you might use me in Christian nursing. Amen*

Notes

Agapē!

God is love. (1 John 4:8)

We memorize Scripture and sing songs praising God for his love. Our prayers are filled with petitions for God's love to penetrate our souls. We seek God's love to reach through our heart and hands, so that we can touch others with this love. When we experience sickness, we pray for the strength of his love to heal and save us. These examples illustrate how we yearn to experience God's love. Central to our faith, is a desire for his love to penetrate each area of our existence.

Yet, God's love, *agapē,* is illusive and hard to fathom. It seems as if the path from understanding love, to living love is long and arduous. Our mysterious journey of faith has barriers, twists and turns, and potholes that seem to prevent us from embracing God's love (Mark 4:13-20; Colossians 2:2). How do we begin to embrace or comprehend the vastness of agapē love?

One way is to go to the source of agapē—God. In order to embrace love, we need to catch a glimpse of God (Psalm 145:3). By exploring various Hebrew names for God, as used in Scripture, we begin to discover the character of God. In 1 Corinthians 13:4-8, we see how the character of God is demonstrated through love. Note the following Hebrew words:

Heavenly Father is patient and kind. Jehovah is not jealous or boastful or proud or rude. Almighty does not demand his own way. Adonai is not irritable, and keeps no record of being wronged. The Most High does not rejoice about injustice but rejoices whenever truth wins out. The LORD never gives up, never loses faith. Elohim is always hopeful and endures through every circumstance. YAHWEH will last forever!

God's Word and his names reveal the vastness of his love and help us absorb the richness of agapē. From hearts overflowing with love we can offer the height, width, depth and length of Christ's love in our nursing care (Ephesians 3:18-19). Christ's love might appear in a tender touch, kind words, or a peaceful presence. Agapē transcends us and reaches our patients with God's love.

Read: 1 Corinthians 13

What attribute of agapē, God's love, is most challenging to you?
Reflecting on 1 Corinthians 13:4-8, consider ways to demonstrate agapē in your nursing care.

Personalize the following prayer by filling in the blanks:
Prayer: *May _____ (insert your name) understand how wide, how long, how high, and how deep Christ's love is; so that _____ (insert your name) may be filled with the fullness of life and power that comes from God! Amen. (Ephesians 3:18-19)*

Notes

Dear Nurse:

I want to take this moment and send you a personal letter recognizing your dedication and work as a nurse in my healthcare system. As I made rounds, I noticed areas where I want to commend you. My heart swelled with pride and honour when you recently spent extra time with a patient. She was facing such a scary, frightening illness; you took time to listen to her fears. I am sure your individual attention brought peace and hope to her challenging situation.

I noticed you collaborate with our team. We have had some rough times; budget cuts and changes in personnel have been frustrating, yet you have taken it in stride. You have willingly worked extra hours when needed to cover for a sick colleague. Also, your input during staff meetings has been invaluable.

Finally, I appreciate your patience with the nursing students who come through our facility. Each one has benefited from your caring attitude and expert knowledge. I know they have learned important skills, relevant nursing care, and professionalism. They may forget some of what they learned, but they will never forget how supportive and caring you were. Your excellence in nursing is a model for future generations.

Sincerely,
God (CEO)

For we are God's masterpiece. He has created us anew in Christ Jesus, so we can do the good things he planned for us long ago. (Ephesians 2:10)

Read: Matthew 16:27, 25:23; Romans 2:6; Revelation 22:12

Add your name to the top of the letter, personalizing the letter to you. Or write yourself a letter from God commending you in the same three areas: patient care, management, mentoring/students, or other areas that reflect your role.

Prayer: *Thank you, God for this letter. Infuse it into my heart, mind and soul so that I can truly believe what you have said to me. Amen. (Isaiah 64:8)*

Notes

Peter's Wisdom

> Stand firm against him [the Devil], and be strong in your faith.
> (1 Peter 5:9)

During the Last Supper, Jesus warned Peter that he would be sifted by Satan (Luke 22:31-34). As the evening continued, Peter repeatedly denied Christ. Peter's rejection of Christ was not quiet; it was vocal and adamant, especially the third denial, after which the rooster crowed. The rooster's morning ritual connected Peter with Jesus' prediction and left Peter facing the nightmarish reality of "sifting," while becoming part of our redemptive story.

Peter felt sifted, distraught, and devoured. Is it any wonder that Peter used the metaphor "devour" to describe Satan's tactic in his first letter? Thankfully, in this same letter, Peter reached out with wisdom: "Stay alert! Watch out for your great enemy, the devil. He prowls around like a roaring lion, looking for someone to devour." (1 Peter 5:8)

Peter encouraged us to "be careful" or stay "alert." This means we can't get complacent about Satan, nor assume he is on vacation. We need to "take a stand against him" and be strong in our faith. This faith is not just filled with words, but is a faith dependent upon Christ (1 John 5:5). The true victor in our war with Satan is Jesus. Peter depended upon Jesus' prayers, "I have pleaded in prayer for you, Simon [Peter] that your faith should not fail" (Luke 22:32). So we, too, depend upon the prayers of Christ (Romans 8:34; John 17: 9-12). The wisdom of Peter is a good reminder for us to stand firm and stay vigilant.

Read: Romans 8:31-39

"I have prayed for you _____ (insert name), that your faith may not fail." How does the reminder that Jesus prays for you boost your confidence during temptations and trials?

Prayer: *Thank you, Jesus, for your prayers of intercession on my behalf. I know you will strengthen and encourage me to stand firm against the evil one. Amen.*

Notes

Global Fellowship

After this I saw a vast crowd, too great to count, from every nation and tribe and people and language, standing in front of the throne and before the Lamb.
(Revelation 7:9)

One of the great benefits of being involved with Nurses Christian Fellowship International (NCFI) is the global fellowship among Christian nurses. There is a sense of connectedness when we hang out with men and women who love Jesus and love nursing. This is especially evident at the International Congress, held every four years. We not only enjoy beautiful scenes, explore new cultures, and gain nursing knowledge, but we experience camaraderie among nurses from different nations, learning how nursing is different, yet the same. Even though we have different jobs in nursing, we have the common bond of caring for patients. As our eyes open, we see international nursing through the hearts of our brothers and sisters in Christ.

As each nurse shares his/her personal struggle, we gain insight into the various hardships in nursing, globally, nationally, and locally. Some nurses need supplies, some are short-staffed, and others have funding deficits. Our hearts ache with nurses who face persecution for their Christian faith. We cry with those experiencing health and/or family concerns.

The NCFI Congress is also a time of blessings. We enjoy a taste of heaven through worship. The diversity of various languages is a foretaste of the miraculous unity of voices when, someday, we will join with the angels and all the nursing saints in heaven, proclaiming praise to Jesus. With fervor and love, unrestricted by our earthly dwelling, our spirits will soar in praise: "Amen! Blessing and glory and wisdom and thanksgiving and honor and power and strength belong to our God forever and ever! Amen." (Revelation 7:12)

Global fellowship is an abundant blessing of NCFI. Through our affiliation with a large multi-member international organization, we build relationships founded on Christ and experience a taste of heaven with our international nursing saints.

Read: Acts 2:41-47

Are you currently part of a fellowship of Christian nurses/healthcare workers? If yes, thank the Lord for the encouragement/support you have received. If not, ask the Lord to connect you with this rich resource.

Prayer: *Heavenly Father, I thank you for the body of Christian nurses whose heart beats with mine as we unite to serve you. Thank you for the blessings we each receive as we gather in your name. Amen.*

Notes

The Wise Nurse

Their [Proverbs] purpose is to teach people to live disciplined and successful lives,
to help them do what is right, just, and fair. (Proverbs 1:2-3)

The book of Proverbs is recognized as a definitive resource for gaining wisdom. Whether seeking moral instruction, shrewdness or discernment, the reader of Proverbs can find helpful hints for godly living. This unique book of the Bible is also a great resource for the judicious and insightful nurse.

Christian nurses are disciples of Christ, who walk with integrity, humility, and embrace the fear of the Lord (22:4). They bind mercy and truth together, exemplifying kindness to the needy and extending graciousness to the poor (3:3, 14:21, 19:17). Whether working in a clinic, hospital, or community, nurses incline their hearts toward understanding (2:1-2). They bend an ear to wisdom while providing instructions to patients and staff (31:26).

Christian nurses abhor evil, pride, arrogance, and falsehoods (8:12-14). They employ prudence to guide their nursing care. They listen to reproof and wise advice from a trusted friend, while ignoring the quarrelsome and wicked (15:31, 26:21). Christian nurses trust the Lord with each step and acknowledge him as the director of their path (3:5-6). Hard work and diligence are good soil for the spiritual fruit of righteousness and love (12:11, 21:21). With reflective hearts, and pure minds Christian nurses can lead others toward gentleness and kindness (27:19, 16:23).

Good looks and riches do not last, but a man or woman who fears the Lord will be greatly praised (31:30-31). Oh, for the good works of nursing to be rewarded and proclaimed in the board rooms!

Read: Review Proverbs citations.

Choose one of the Proverbs discussed and apply to your nursing practice.

Prayer: *O Lord, May I trust in you with all my heart and not depend on my own understanding. May I seek your wisdom in all I do, so that you may direct my path. Amen. (Proverbs 3:5-6)*

Notes

No Nurses in Heaven!

He will swallow up death forever! The Sovereign LORD will wipe away all tears.
(Isaiah 25:8)

As healthcare workers, we have dedicated our gifts and talents to caring for the sick, the disabled, and the mentally ill. Our nursing service is a calling or ministry, and we feel privileged to be appointed by God to care for his children. I think I can speak for both you and me in saying, we have both joy and confidence in doing the Lord's work. Fused with our delight in service is the distress we experience when we witness the anguish of those in our care. We yearn for a time without sickness, disease, and death; a time when there is no bad news to tell families, nor painful treatments to administer. We long for a time when, instead of holding a hand to comfort, we hold a hand to celebrate.

Thankfully, our yearning will be fulfilled in heaven. Revelation 21:4 reminds us that a time is coming when there will be no more death, sorrow, or pain. Jesus will personally wipe away every tear from our patients' eyes. Pain and suffering will be gone forever.

In addition to seeing Jesus face-to-face, I am excited to go to a place where there are no hospitals, no clinics, and no nurses! Hallelujah! We will suddenly be unemployed, our services no longer be needed. This is the good news of the gospel for our patients, their family, and for all healthcare workers. Someday, there will come a time when healthy bodies, minds, and souls will live for eternity without the fear of disease, the heart break of disability, nor the slow deterioration of ageing (1 Corinthians 15:52-55).

We do not know what the Lord has planned for us to do in heaven, however we do know we can anticipate an eternity without the need for nurses!

Read: 1 Corinthians 15:35-58; Revelation 21:1-7

What do you look forward to when you think of "no nurses in heaven"?

Prayer: *Lord, my heart is heavy with all the suffering I witness. Thank you for the promise of an eternity without pain! Amen.*

Notes

"Come quickly, Lord"

The Spirit and the bride say, "Come." Let each one who hears this say, "Come."
(Revelation 22:17)

By anticipating a place without sickness, we are prompted to expectantly watch for the return of Jesus Christ. This return is based on Jesus' promises to the disciples, "Do not be troubled, I go to prepare a place for you and I will return to take you there to live with me" (John 14:1-3; Matthew 24:29-31). In Christian theology we call this event, The Second Coming. Even though the timing of the event is unknown, we have a description of Jesus' impending arrival:

For the Lord himself will come down from heaven with a commanding shout, with the voice of the archangel, and with the trumpet call of God. First, the believers who have died will rise from their graves. Then, together with them, we who are still alive and remain on the earth will be caught up in the clouds to meet the Lord in the air. Then we will be with the Lord forever (1 Thessalonians 4:16-17).

Just as the first century believers did, we ask, "When will Jesus return?" The wait seems endless, especially as violence spreads throughout our countries and devastating diseases and plagues cause death and disability.

It is easy to become discouraged. Our impatience alternates between demanding *"When*, Lord?" and apathetically murmuring, *"Whateve*r, Lord." Neither response expresses expectant hope. As we anticipate the return of Christ, we can inspire our fellow believers to stay steadfast, trusting God with the details. At the same time as we desire our Lord to hasten and "come" quickly, we can hold onto Christ's assurance, "Yes. I am coming soon" (Revelation 22:20).

Read: Revelation 22

How can we stay steadfast in our faithful service while praying, "Come quickly, Lord Jesus"?

Prayer: *We wait for the happy fulfillment of our hope in the glorious appearing of our great God and Saviour, Jesus Christ. Come quickly! Amen. (Titus 2:13)*

Notes

Dementia for Today

Instead, let the Spirit renew your thoughts and attitudes. (Ephesians 4:23)

Many of us are faced with the possibility of acquiring the dreaded diagnosis of Alzheimer disease or dementia. It is scary to think that growing older might bring confusion and memory loss, or a time when we will not recognize our loved ones, nor be able to care for ourselves. Our personal history, once filled with precious memories, might be lost amidst a tangle of neurons. On the other hand, memory loss found through the transformational healing of Christ is attainable today through forgiveness (Psalm 103:12).

Imagine the miracle of forgetting those painful events or the people who caused us harm. The hurtful details and faces would be erased, deleted, and purged from our memory. Wouldn't it be great to clear out the reminders of our past sins and transgressions to free up brain space for more productive use—or to melt those mistaken misadventures we chose early in our youth? Wouldn't it be nice to use an eraser to wipe them away? And what about those traumatic events in our lives, where our Christian journey included sorrow and pain? Using a gardening tool on our memory, we could pull out the weeds of pain and grief, while leaving the strong roots of trust and faith.

Miraculously this memory loss happens today through the completed work of forgiveness. Throughout Scripture we are repeatedly assured that our past sins, transgressions, and wayward paths have been erased (Jeremiah 31:34; Psalm 103:12; Colossians 1:14). Furthermore, we are welcomed into the holiest of holies, trusting in the intercession of Christ's blood (Hebrews 9:12-15). Not that forgetfulness is a good attribute, but let's welcome some memory loss as the Lord cleanses our minds of things best left forgotten (Matthew 6:14-15, 18:21-22; 1 John 1:9).

Read: Hebrews 10:1-22

Are there event(s) from your past that linger in your memories, in need of forgiveness? If so, allow God to replace those memories of yesterday with the joy and peace of today.

Prayer: *Thank you, Jesus, for providing the necessary sacrifice for a redemptive life with the Father. Open my heart to ways I can live out your forgiveness, especially toward those who have caused me harm. Amen.*

Notes

Storehouse of Bread

The grass withers and the flower fades, but the word of our God stands forever.
(Isaiah 40:8)

Years ago, while volunteering to provide spiritual care at a nursing home, I met an inspirational resident. She was an elderly lady who kindly greeted me when I entered her room. I introduced myself and told her I was with a local church and wanted to chat with her. She was thrilled. Within the last year she had developed a neurodegenerative disease, rendering her completely paralyzed. In the process of her disease, she had acquired a large decubitus/wound on her sacrum and was now bedbound. She was not allowed to sit in a chair, nor raise the head-of-the bed more than 30 degrees.

Even in her physical condition, she was cheerful and hopeful. She shared with me how she prayed for all the staff and a few of the residents she had met. She kept a stack of encouragement cards on her table and shared them with everyone entering her room. We both knew Jesus was using her as a loving witness in the facility.

I asked her how I could encourage her and what she needed. On one hand, she missed reading her Bible, yet she had noticed a strange phenomenon. As she lay motionless in bed, Scripture filled her mind. The verses and passages weren't recent teachings or sermons; she hadn't attended church or Bible study since her illness. She explained it like this, "All those Scripture verses and passages that I memorized through the years are now bathing my heart, mind, and soul." She was amazed, as was I.

At a time when she was cut off from her "daily bread," the Lord brought slices to feed her spirit from the storehouses of her mind. We both praised and thanked God for his eternal presence. I commended her for her former obedience to memorizing God's words.

Even though I came weekly and read the Bible to her, she imparted saintly wisdom to me. As my older sister-in-Christ, she reminded me of the importance of storing up God's Word in my heart, so that I will always have it when I need it most (Psalm 119:105).

Read: Psalm 119:89-105

Psalm 119 shares various ways God's law, words, and commands enrich our lives. Peruse the passage, taking note of how God can speak to you through Scripture.

Prayer: *O Lord, I thank for your Word that guides my life and communicates your ways to me. I also thank you for the fellowship of believers who enrich my life with godly wisdom. Amen.*

Notes

Drops of Kindness

Since you excel in so many ways—in your faith, your gifted speakers, your knowledge, your enthusiasm, and your love from us—I want you to excel also in this gracious act of giving. (2 Corinthians 8:7)

One of the challenges in nursing is our work environment. Whether it is conflict with colleagues, strained relationship with administration, or the chronic stress of healthcare, living out our faith at work can be difficult. A useful, effective way to bring the love of Christ to work is through simple acts of kindness. Simple doesn't imply easy. Like the old proverb/story that says, "Don't pray for patience, for the Lord will give you lots of practice," the same is true for kindness. It is easy to say, "I will be kinder today," until you get out of bed and the day begins. Still, simple acts of kindness are small drops of mercy that can be sprinkled all around. These scattered, purposeful acts point to the loving, graceful God we serve. Here are few suggestions for scattering kindness:
--assist with a colleague's workload (patients, paperwork, etc.) without recompense
--buy coffee/tea/lunch for a colleague or staff member
--say a kind word, an encouragement, or a heart-felt accolade
--listen empathetically (without advice), to a person's stress or worry
--bring a favorite dish or treat to share
--purchase flowers or other small gifts to say "Thank you"

At the heart of kindness, is your individual heart—reaching out to others with authenticity and caring. These simple drops of kindness, combine with the purposeful presence of the Holy Spirit to exemplify the living Christ for all to see (Ephesians 5:1).

Read: Matthew 5:43-48; Colossians 3:12-17

Spend time praying specifically for a colleague, to whom you can bring drops of kindness.

Prayer: *Lord, through your loving-kindness, I have been abundantly blessed. Help me find meaningful ways to share your presence with my colleagues. Amen.*

Notes

Sealed, Secured, and Sanctified

And when you believed in Christ, he identified you as his own by giving you the Holy Spirit. (Ephesians 1:13)

An amazing miracle happens every time a person comes to salvation through faith in Jesus Christ: that person receives a mark or seal. In an instant, someone not only receives righteousness through the forgiveness of sins, he also receives the identification of Holy Spirit (2 Corinthians 1:22). This is a seal of ownership as children of God (Ephesians 1:13-14). Just like the wax seal placed on documents in ancient times, the mark identifies and indicates ownership. Thus, the owner or originator of the document would "protect" the document. Security and ownership were important as the document traveled from sender to receiver.

So too, the Holy Spirit marks Christians. Like ancient documents were sealed, we are identified with Christ, secured as God's, and protected by the Almighty (1 Corinthians 6:19-20). This marking, unseen by human eyes, provides proof of our true identity in Christ Jesus.

The seal also indicates our sanctification, through the indwelling Holy Spirit. This eternal mark signifies our righteousness. With our past wiped clean, and our future guaranteed, we can stand in confidence that we are sanctified as the Lord's precious child, even when we are tempted to feel unworthy and deficient (Romans 8:15).

Let's rejoice in the security of our inheritance until the day of our redemption, when God will identify us through his holy seal, and usher us into his presence. Praise the Lord!

Read: Romans 8:14-30

Is there an aspect of your relationship with God through the Holy Spirit that you sometimes doubt or feel uncomfortable about: sealed, secured, sanctified?

Prayer: *Lord Jesus, help me to live securely as a sanctified son/daughter of the Most High. Amen.*

Notes

A Sabbath Rest

On the seventh day God had finished his work of creation, so he rested from all
his work. (Genesis 2:2)

The demands of nursing are usually hard work, managing multiple
responsibilities, and, for those who work in hospitals, crazy shifts. Nurses also
care for their families and many volunteer in their churches and communities. I
wonder if Mark had nurses in mind when he wrote, "Then Jesus said, 'Let's go off
by ourselves to a quiet place and rest awhile.' He said this because there were so
many people coming and going that Jesus and his apostles didn't even have time
to eat." (Mark 6:31)

Like Jesus, we spend our days healing, teaching, and supervising, with barely
any time to eat or use the restroom. Even when we have an opportunity to slip
away for a quick bite or a moment to gather our thoughts, we sometimes are
pulled back to our duties, with even more pressing tasks and patient care.

Thus we need a Sabbath rest—a day sometime during the week to push the
pause button on our responsibilities. Sabbath rest allows time for self-care and
enjoyment of God's blessings. It is possible to lay aside work and ministry
responsibilities for one day. The challenge usually comes with altering our duties.
Through careful planning and coordination, modifications can be made to ensure
everyone enjoys a day filled with togetherness[2]. The goal is not to create more
havoc for our personal life (Mark 2:27); the goal is to discover a balance of work
and rest, so that we may be rejuvenated and refreshed to serve those entrusted to
our care. The Lord knew we would face the temptation of workaholism, thus one
of his foundational commandments—keep the Sabbath—was given for our good.
The Sabbath is a reflection of the balance our Creator modeled for us.

Read: Exodus 20:8-11; Mark 6:30-34

Make a commitment to designate a day of rest where you stop work and ministry
responsibilities and minimize household duties for refreshment and rejuvenation.

Prayer: *Father God, you created the Sabbath as a time to rest in your presence. Help me to
recognize its importance and to practice this ancient ritual in my life today. Amen.*

Notes

A Noun or a Verb?

> Jesus felt sorry [compassion] for them and touched their eyes. Instantly they could
> see! Then they followed him. (Matthew 20:34)

There is a lot of talk in my country (England) about "compassion,"
particularly in relation to nursing and why people perceive that there is a lack of
compassion in the profession. But what does compassion really mean? Most Bible
translations use the English "compassion" (literally meaning, "to suffer
alongside") to translate several different words in the Bible – none of which has
so simple a meaning.

In this quoted passage, the Greek word translated "moved with compassion"
is *splagchnizomai,* which literally means 'to be moved in one's innards' – either the
bowels or the organs of the rib-cage[3]. It is an expression of the most visceral,
physical response to the needs and suffering of others. When Jesus hears the pleas
of the blind men to have their sight restored, he is moved to his guts. But when
we see Jesus profoundly moved here, he does not stop with feelings. He acts,
decisively and firmly, to address the need that he sees, and heals both men there
and then. Compassion in the Bible is a verb, not a noun – like love, it only means
something if it leads to decisive action.

In nursing, we are told to keep a professional distance, not to get involved.
However, having true compassion means we need to be open to the pain and
suffering of our patients, at any level, and be willing and able to be truly moved,
and to respond decisively. Responding may mean sorting out displaced pillows to
make someone comfortable, ensuring that appropriate analgesia is provided on
schedule, or simply being present with a person in the most profound and
inexpressible distress. If we are not moved and spurred to action by our patient's
need, how can we be truly compassionate?

Read: Matthew 9:35-38; 20:29-34; Luke 7:11-17

In what tangible ways might you respond compassionately to a patient, staff, or
student in distress?

Prayer, *Lord Jesus, help us to not only empathize with your children, but guide us in acting
with compassion. Amen.*

Steve Fouch
CMF Head of Nursing Ministries
Chair, NCFI European Committee

Notes

P Purpose & Plan

> You are the great and powerful God, the LORD Almighty. You have all wisdom
> and do great and mighty miracles. (Jeremiah 32:18-19)

An acrostic is a form of writing in which the first letter of each line in the text spells out a word or a message. The next 13 reflections are an acrostic from the word **PERSEVERANCE(A)**. I pray each reflection strengthens your faithful walk with Jesus Christ.

During a turbulent time of Israel's history, the Lord told Jeremiah to buy property. This was an unusual request. Jeremiah had already told the king of Judah that Nebuchadnezzar, the king of Babylon, was on his way to capture and destroy Jerusalem.

Despite his doubt about the wisdom of God's plan, out of obedience to God, Jeremiah purchased the property. Then Jeremiah prayed. He started by praising God for his great providence as the Creator. "O Sovereign LORD! You have made the heavens and earth by your great power. Nothing is too hard for you! You are loving and kind to thousands" (32:17-18). Next, Jeremiah's prayer revealed what God had done in the past. "You performed miraculous signs and wonders in the land of Egypt—things still remembered to this day" (32:20).

The Lord answered Jeremiah's prayer and told him the purpose and plan for the land purchase—to communicate God's continued faithfulness to the Israelites (32:35-44). Even though calamity would come to the Israelites, God was still in control and had a plan for their future.

Just like Jerusalem, God has a plan for nursing and healthcare. At times we become discouraged and only see the current chaos or problems. When we struggle in our faith or are anxious about the future, we can come to God in prayer. We can remember his greatness, the prayers he has previously answered, and trust in his plans for nursing. God is the same yesterday, today, and tomorrow (Hebrews 13:8).

Read: Jeremiah 32:6-44

What concerns do you have for your ministry or work in nursing?
How can your past experience(s) with God keep you focused on his purpose and plan?

Prayer: *Father God, I praise you for your great works in nursing. Help me to walk in faith today and tomorrow following your plans for nursing. Amen.*

Notes

E Energy (Koach)

He [God] gives power to those who are tired and worn out. (Isaiah 40:29)

When we think of perseverance, we can't help but think of how fatigue and exhaustion interferes with all we want to do for Jesus. Nurses, as well as other healthcare professionals become weary from the physical demands of work. Repositioning patients, managing multiple tasks, and supervising staff can be tiring. We can also become drained from the emotional and mental work required to care for the suffering and dying. In addition to our roles as nurses, we are parents, spouses, and members of our communities and churches. These responsibilities and commitments add to our already drained body and mind. At times, we feel pushed beyond our limits of strength and endurance

Isaiah 40:29 states, "He [the Lord] gives power to those who are tired and worn out." Other words used for tired are weary, feeble, or faint. The original Hebrew word used here for "power" is *koach*, which translates as the strength, power, or might of humans and animals. *Koach* is also used to describe the power of angels and God[4]. Wow, the strength of angels—this sounds like a great strength to have! Most of the time when we see power or strength noted in the Bible, we limit it to spiritual power or strength for our faith. Yet, it can also speak of vigor or muscle strength.

Next time you are exhausted and needing a boost of strength, don't reach for caffeine. Instead, ask the Lord for his power and might (2 Samuel 22:33). Ask God not only to give you strength for your faith, but to give you energy to care for one more patient, teach one more class, and hold one more hand (Philippians 4:13).

Read: Isaiah 40:12-31

Which type of strength are you more likely to pray for: emotional, mental, spiritual, or physical? How are each of these strengths important to your perseverance?

Prayer: *Father God, teach me to depend on you for all the strength(s) I need to persevere. Amen.*

Notes

R Resources

"For there are more on our side than on theirs!" (2 Kings 6:16)

Elisha, like many of the Old Testament prophets, had a price on his head. Elisha informed the King of Israel of the movements of the King of Syria (Aram), and so Israel found escape. Finally, the King of Syria discovered where Elisha was hiding and sent an army to surround the city.

Elisha's servant rose early in the morning, only to discover the Syrian army had them surrounded. He panicked. Elisha not only encouraged his servant, "For there are more on our side than on theirs" (2 Kings 6:16), he prayed for the Lord to open his servant's eyes, so that he too could see the Lord's army surrounding them.

The difference between Elisha and his servant was the ability to see the resources the Lord had provided. Elisha trusted the Lord and could see the army protecting him. He wasn't stressed about tomorrow or worried about next month. Like other prophets, Elisha lived from resource to resource, trusting God to provide.

As we persevere to stay faithful to the Lord's work, God has already provided all we need. Scripture, both Old and New Testaments, are rich in examples, illustrations, and words of truth that can encourage and strengthen us in ministry (Matthew 4:4). We also have an international fellowship of nurses praying for each individual nurse—that is both *you* and me! And, above all else, we have the living Christ dwelling in each of us, opening our eyes to the Lord's army surrounding us! (Luke 24:31, 36)

Read: 2 Kings 6:8-33

How are you encouraged by the image of Lord's army surrounding you?

Prayer: *Lord Jesus, many times I am spiritual blind to your rich resources. Open my eyes to your abundance and the army that protects me. Amen.*

Notes

S Song of the Suffering

> My God, my God! Why have you forsaken me? Why do you remain so distant?
> Why do you ignore my cries for help? (Psalm 22:1)

Sometimes perseverance includes a season or period filled with pain, grief, and/or fear. These unwelcomed emotions and thoughts bind around heart and soul. We can pour out our hearts to God, disclosing our deepest aches and doubts. This honest reflection can occur through prayer, song, or meditation.

In Psalm 22, David openly shared his deepest feelings and thoughts with God: "Every day I call to you, my God, but you do not answer. Every night you hear my voice, but I find no relief" (v. 2). In anguish he described a loss of self-image, "I am a worm not a man" (v. 6). In a lowly state, mocked and despised, David moaned, "My strength has dried up like sunbaked clay. My tongue sticks to the roof of my mouth" (v. 15). Through the physical pain of depression David cried out, "All my bones are out of joint. My heart is like wax" (v. 14). David openly blamed God for his agony, "You have laid me in the dust and left me for dead" (v. 15).

Intermixed with personal anguish, David received affirmations from the Lord, "You have been my God from the moment I was born" (v. 10). As well, David received reminders of the Lord's faithfulness to himself and others, "Praise the LORD...For he has not ignored the suffering of the needy. He has not turned and walked away. He has listened to their cries for help" (v. 23-24).

Like David, we can bring our deepest pain during dark moments of perseverance to God's throne room. Our Father in heaven is already well-acquainted with our pain and suffering. Our Lord will sprinkle drops of sweet honey of himself, reaffirming the authenticity of his faithfulness for us (Psalm 119:103; Hebrews 13:5-6).

Read: Psalm 22

Do you feel comfortable sharing your intimate, deep thoughts and feelings with God? If not, explore personal/religious barriers that prevent you from following David's example.

Prayer: *O Lord, help me come to you and honestly share my distress, disappointment, and despair so that I may gain strength to persevere. Amen.*

Notes

E Equipped Abundantly

[God said], "I want the people of Israel to build me a sacred residence where I can live among them. You must make this Tabernacle and its furnishings exactly according to the plans I will show you." (Exodus 25:8-9)

The explicit instructions the Lord gave to Moses for building the tabernacle in Exodus chapters 25-40 are amazing! The tabernacle was truly an engineering feat that was not only functional and ornately beautiful, it was transportable. Moses received clear, specific architectural plans, and acquired all the supplies from the Israelites (Exodus 25:1-9, 35:21). In response to a "stirring in their heart," the women brought their jewelry, fine linen and yarn, as well as their skills in sewing and spinning (Exodus 35:20-25). And, the men brought animal skins, precious gems, metal, and acacia wood.

For the intricate, elaborate work required, the Lord filled Bezalel "with the Spirit of God, giving him great wisdom, ability, and expertise in all kinds of crafts" (v. 31). Bezalel was uniquely gifted in carving wood, working with gold, and cutting and setting gemstones. Both Bezalel and Oholiab were given the ability to teach others the skills of master craftsmen and designers (35:30-35).

The Lord provided for every minute detail needed for the completion of the tabernacle: plans, supplies, experts, teachers, builders, and others. Just as the Lord equipped the Israelites, the Lord will equip us with everything we need in nursing.

So, what do you need at this very moment? Do you need money for school, clinic supplies, and/or housing? Do you need specific support and direction for your ministry, job, or career? Many times our needs guide our hearts and spirits to take a step in faith for Christ. Maybe your needs are more personal and faith-related, such as trust, patience, courage, or hope! What is essential for you to continue persevering for Christ in nursing?

Our God is a God of specifics, and he promises to equip us with all we need to do his work (Ephesians 4:11-12; Philippians 4:19). He will not only provide what we need, but he may surprise us with an abundance. Moses commanded the people to stop bringing more gifts! "You have already given more than enough!" (Exodus 36:6-7). Hallelujah!

Read: Exodus 25:1-9, 31:1-11, 35:20-36:7

Write down your specific needs; pray for them daily for 30 days.

Prayer: *Thank you, Lord, for equipping me for nursing. Help me to see your abundance—Hallelujah! Amen.*

Notes

V Victory Promised

Hebron still belongs to descendants of Caleb son of Jephunneh the Kenizzite because he wholeheartedly followed the LORD, the God of Israel. (Joshua 14:14)

At the edge of the Promised Land, Moses sent a leader from each of the 12 tribes (Numbers 13). For forty days the group of young men spied on their future home: Would it be habitable? What were the people like? Upon their return, the representatives brought pomegranates, figs, and grapes, along with a detailed report to Moses and the Israelites. They shared how Canaan was full of "milk and honey" but they were doubtful and fearful because they had seen the powerful "giants" and the walled cities (v. 28-29, 33). Caleb and Joshua disagreed with their fellow representatives (Numbers 13:30; 14:6). Caleb boldly reported, "Let's go…. We can certainly conquer it!" (Numbers 13:30). Unfortunately, the other representatives spread discouraging words and fear, which persuaded the Israelites to refuse to move forward and take possession of their Promised Land.

Forty years later, after all the original spies had died, except Caleb and Joshua, it was once again time to take the land. At 85, Caleb was just as confident and ready for battle, "Now, as you can see, the LORD has kept me alive... So give me the hill country that the LORD promised me" (Joshua 14:10-12). He had patiently waited for this moment. Yet, Caleb knew victory wouldn't be found in his courage. Victory was in the Lord, "If the LORD is with me, I will drive them out of the land, just as the LORD said" (v. 12).

As we struggle with persevering in nursing, Caleb provides an excellent example: a) stay faithful and patient while enduring challenges; b) refuse to get bitter and angry at life's delaying circumstances; and c) maintain focus on God's promise of victory. Don't let discouragement and fear lead us to abandon our resolve for victory in nursing!

Read: Numbers 13; Joshua 14

What does victory look like for your ministry/work in nursing?
What struggles/barriers make you doubt God's promise?

Prayer: *Oh Lord, keep me steadfast on your promises and thank you for allowing me the privilege of sharing in your victory. Amen.*

Notes

E Enthusiasm

At last the wall was completed to half its original height around the entire city, for the people had worked very hard. (Nehemiah 4:6).

Nehemiah was a Jewish man who worked as a cupbearer for the King of Persia around 450 B.C.. He had heard that his fellow Jews, who had returned to Jerusalem, were in great trouble, and without any defense as their beloved city was in ruins. The news broke Nehemiah's heart. So, he fasted and prayed to God. Through a series of events, the Lord led Nehemiah to go to Jerusalem and rebuild the wall surrounding the city, so that, once again the wall would provide protection for his kinsmen residing in the city (Nehemiah 1:1—2:8).

Sanballat and Tobiah were in opposition to rebuilding the wall and ridiculed Nehemiah and the workers. As the leader, Nehemiah knew discouragement and ridicule would chip away at the workers' resolve to complete the wall. Typical for Nehemiah, he prayed to God. The result was a renewed resolve and enthusiasm of the workforce (Nehemiah 4:6-15). Nehemiah and the workers continued to face opposition to the rebuilding efforts. Instead of becoming discouraged, sidetracked, or fearful, Nehemiah strived for excellence, completing the wall in 52 days! (Nehemiah 6:15).

Nehemiah is a great example for nursing[5]. He faced opposition to God's purpose, yet stayed focused and determined. It is easy to get discouraged and disheartened when we bump against opposition. Nehemiah provides a great example of communicating with God through prayer and depending on him to keep us dedicated to his purpose.

Read: Nehemiah 1:1—2:10, 4:1-6

Are you currently discouraged/disheartened?
How might Nehemiah's experience bring a new resolve and passion for nursing/life?

Prayer: *Father God, I confess that at times I feel discouraged, especially when I face opposition. Help me look to you for a renewed focus that is filled with a fervor for you! Amen.*

Notes

R Rally Partners

[Nehemiah said], "The work is very spread out, and we are widely separated from
each other along the wall." (Nehemiah 4:19)

At every turn, Nehemiah faced opposition to rebuilding the wall. There were
times the workers were so intimidated and frightened they carried their swords
and shields while they worked. They even took their weapons to get water and
when they slept (Nehemiah 4:23). Nehemiah could see that they were not only
afraid, but they needed support to complete the task.

Nehemiah assigned guards, equipped more workers with weapons, and
divided workers into two shifts. This way, the workers could defend themselves
while completing the wall. Yes, the workers' morale still lagged and they struggled
to complete their assigned sections (v. 12) So, Nehemiah posted a trumpet player
who would sound an alarm not only as a warning, but as a rally shout! When the
workers heard the blast of the trumpet, they were to gather together and shout,
"Our God will fight for us!" (Nehemiah 4:20).

This shout of praise not only created a sense of security for the workers, it
took their minds off the fear of the enemy, the hard work of building the wall,
and the isolation of the individual worker. It helped them join as rally partners.
Together they would remember and focus on Yahweh—the One who goes
before them, the One who finds solutions, and the One who connected them
with each other (Deuteronomy 1:30).

At this moment you may feel alone, overwhelmed by difficulties, or
burdened by overwork, but God provides rally partners in nursing. Christian
nurses can come alongside one another and give a shout of praise! At the same
time, we each can be a rally partner for someone else. Together, we can encourage
one another with a shout of praise!

Read: Nehemiah 4

What specific shout do you need to hear from a rally partner?
How could you be a rally partner for your nursing unit, clinic, or ministry?

Prayer: *Thank you, Jesus, for your shouts of encouragement that you bring into my ministry!
You are truly my Rally Partner! Amen.*

Notes

A Adversity's Purpose

I went away full, but the LORD has brought me home empty. Why should you call me Naomi when the LORD has caused me to suffer and the Almighty has sent such tragedy? (Ruth 1:21)

Many Christians are familiar with the story of Ruth, found in the book with the same name. The story is of a wonderful Jewish courtship between Ruth and her kinsman redeemer, Boaz. Yet, the prologue to their love story is the adversity experienced by Naomi.

In a span of 10 years, Naomi had lost her husband and two sons. She then made a long journey back to her home in Judea. She arrived in her home town of Bethlehem and was greeted by old friends. Her response is filled with despondency and hopelessness, "Don't call me Naomi [which means *pleasant*].... Instead call me Mara" [which means *bitter*] (v. 20). Years before, she and her family had left a famine-ridden Bethlehem with the hope of a growing family and prosperity. To return as a widow, and without sons, was seen as a destiny of shame and poverty. Picking-up fallen grain became her only means of food. Even though Naomi was bitter, depressed, and devastated, she persevered.

Like Naomi, our lives can be full of hardships, death, and suffering. We live in a fallen world filled with evil; pain and suffering are part of our human experience. Even as children of God, we are not immune to global misery. It is important to keep in mind that the Lord doesn't cause pain and suffering, yet he accomplishes his purpose through adversity.

We may not always know God's purpose in our distress. Naomi didn't know during those dark periods that the Saviour of the world would come through her! Through the union of her distant relative, Boaz, with the widow of her dead son, Ruth, a son, Obed, was born. Obed was the grandfather of Kind David. Twenty-eight generations later, Jesus Christ was born of this lineage (Ruth 4:16; Matthew 1:5-16).

Not only does God care about our pain and suffering, his mighty purpose is being worked out through it (Romans 8:28-29). We have no idea what purpose is being worked out through our adversity (Job 36:15; Jeremiah 29:11). Yet, we do know we will experience Jesus in a new, faith-building way (Romans 5:3-4).

Read: Ruth 1, 4

Are you currently experiencing adversity? If so, how can God's promise of building your faith bring you comfort and hope?

Prayer: *Father God, I know that you cause everything to work together for the good of those who love you. Help me to open my heart and seek you when I feel the farthest away. Amen*

Notes

N Navigating Presence

The LORD guided them by a pillar of cloud during the day and a pillar of fire at night. (Exodus 13:21)

God performed many amazing and dramatic miracles for the Israelites during their great Exodus out of Egypt. He guided their every step across the wilderness through his continued presence as a visible cloud and pillar of fire. Whether it was day or night, stormy or calm, the Israelites just looked forward to find the Lord's presence directing their steps.

There is a richness of knowledge demonstrated in this amazing relationship between God and his people. We have the same guiding presence to navigate our lives: Jesus Christ through the indwelling Holy Spirit. Just as the cloud guided the Israelites through the rough, difficult desert life, Jesus goes before us, guiding and lighting our path. At times our pillar of fire confuses our enemies, just as it did for the Israelites' enemies (Exodus 14:24). Later, when the Israelites built the Tabernacle, they witnessed the cloud come and rest on the Tabernacle, signifying Yahweh's active presence and blessing.

At times, we face both spiritual and human opposition to our obedience to the Lord. No matter how seemingly dark and alone we may feel, Jesus lights the darkness and provides all we need to remain steadfast through our trials and tribulations (Exodus 14:19; Deuteronomy 1:33). Even when we are at our worst and feel alienated from God, he is truly only a word away from us. We just need to look to Jesus to find our light (John 1:4; 2 Corinthians 4:6). His presence will continuously lead and guide us through our desert experiences.

Read: Exodus 40:34-38; Deuteronomy 1:29-33

What characteristic(s) of the Lord's continued presence do you currently need? Write them out as a prayer request to the Lord.

Prayer: *Father God, I desperately need your navigation during times of difficulty. Open my heart to your Presence, which lights my way. Amen.*

Notes

C Courage

He prayed three times a day, just as he had always done, giving thanks to his God.
(Daniel 6:10)

One of the necessary attributes needed to persevere is courage. Courage is bravery in continuing against adversity, being resolute, staying faithful to our calling; being determined; continuing amidst physical pain and suffering, as well as fearlessly witnessing for Christ in hostile environments. To most of us, courage looks too big and too bold to embrace, yet the Lord builds our courage slowly, persistently, as we walk along our journey.

An Old Testament example of courage is Daniel. He lived a life built on courage. Any perusal of his life demonstrates Daniel's steps in courage, starting as a young man. As a young man, he was on guard against practices in Babylon that were contradictory to his faith (1:8-16). Daniel stepped out bravely to trust God's revelation to him and was able to accurately reveal and interpret Nebuchadnezzar's dream. This not only saved his life, it saved all the wise leaders from death (2:1-49). Daniel's courage was most severely tested when he defiantly continued his prayer practices, open and seen by all. He didn't allow the fear of death to change his commitment and obedience to God (6:1-28). He willingly faced death, resigning himself to death, if need be (6:19-21).

As we persevere for Christ at work, at home, and in our communities, our faithful brother, Daniel, encourages us with his life's testimony. He stood strong for what he believed and the Lord used him for mighty things. He was a counselor to kings, a wise leader, and a prophet. His dreams, visions, and discussions with the angel Gabriel left us with words anticipating the return of Christ. Daniel lived out instruction to persevere with courage; he was firm in his faith, strong against opposition, and persistent in prayer (1 Corinthians 16:13; Romans 12:12).

Read: Daniel 1; 2, 6

What events in Daniel's life fills you with courage to preserve?

Prayer: *Thank you, Lord, for the testimony of Daniel and other saints who provide me with holy examples of courage. Help me to be brave and steadfast in living a faithful life. Amen.*

Notes

E Eternal Nursing Crown

"As for you, go your way until the end. You will rest, and then at the end of the days, you will rise again to receive the inheritance set aside for you."
(Daniel 12:13)

The previous reflection allowed us to witness courage in Daniel's life. We also noticed how God affirmed Daniel's faithfulness with a promised inheritance. Daniel's reward for his enduring, obedient life is the same as ours—eternal life with the King of Kings, and Lord of Lords.

"Look, the home of God is now among his people. He will live with them, and they will be his people! God himself will be with them" (Revelation 21:3). This is the new kingdom Jesus promised the disciples, a place where we will dwell with the all the saints, including Daniel (Matthew 26:29, Revelation 1:6, 5:9-10).

Jesus, along with the writers of the New Testament, also encourages us with the promise of rewards or crowns (Matthew 5:12; 1 Corinthians 3:8). In fact, Scripture clearly teaches a reward or crown for those who stand firm during trials and temptations (James 1:12).

I have always wondered if our nursing crown will look different. Will it have an empathetic heart or a symbol of comforting hands? I doubt our crown will have much "bling." Most Christian nurses are humble and gracious and wouldn't want anything too bright or showy. I imagine that our crown would be simple and functional, though. Similar to the nursing caps of our past, they could be clean, pressed, and worn with dignity and honor.

However our crown looks, we have the assurance that we have done well and completed the work Christ has given us. "I have fought a good fight, I have finished the race, and I have remained faithful. And now the prize awaits me—the crown of righteousness that the Lord, the righteous Judge, will give me on that great day of his return. And the prize is not just for me but for all who eagerly look forward to his glorious return" (2 Timothy 4:7-8).

At that time, as faithful servants we will lay our crowns at the feet of our Jesus, knowing all we are, and everything we did came from him (Revelation 4:10-11).

Read: Hebrews 10:35-38--11

Hebrews 11 lists faithful believers, for example: "It is by faith that Noah/Abraham". Then, the verses list their actions built an ark/obeyed (vv. 7, 8). Add your name to the list of faithful Christians, by filling in the blanks: It is by faith, _____ [insert your name] and then list your role/duties/etc. in nursing _____.

Prayer: *Father God, it is easy to get discouraged and forget that you have promised me more than I can imagine. Not that I want to focus on my reward, Lord, but encourage me through recognizing my service to you with my nursing talents. Amen.*

Notes

Adoration

> I came naked from my mother's womb, and I will be naked when I leave. The LORD gave me what I had, and the LORD has taken it away. Praise the name of the LORD! (Job 1:21)

Job received a trio of tragic news about his ranch. Through three successive messengers Job learns that all his livestock, ranch hands, and shepherds are dead (1:15-17). Even as Job grappled with this profound tragedy, a fourth messenger brings horrific details of how a wind storm destroyed a house, and subsequently killed all his children (1:18-20). As an expression of profound grief, Job tears his robe and shaves his head. His despair rises as praise and solidarity to Yahweh, "The LORD gave me what I had, and the LORD has taken it away. Praise the name of the LORD!"(Job 1:21).

As Job is reeling with grief, he develops a horrible skin condition, boils that erupt from his head to his toes. Amidst the ashes of his previous life, Job scratches his sores with a piece of broken pottery and continues to proclaim: "Should we accept only good things from the hand of God and never anything bad?"(Job 2:10).

At each junction of loss, devastation, and suffering, Job resolved to praise God. He didn't seek to answer the why's or to discover the how's of his tragedy. Nor did he expect, as a righteous man of God, special favour. Instead, he adored and honored God as the sovereign "I AM"(Exodus 3:14; John 8:58).

It is hard to imagine how we can adore God when we are overwhelmed with devastation, suffering, and death. Yet we can, for we choose to praise God (2 Corinthians 11:24-31). It doesn't mean we skip the grieving or the mourning. Instead our pain and distress is united with the sovereignty of God (2 Corinthians 4:8-12; 1 Chronicles 29:15).

Read: 2 Corinthians 4:8-12

Do you have a praise song, Bible passage, or verse that encourages your faith during difficult times? If not, seek the Lord and search scripture for encouraging verse(s).

Prayer: *"O LORD, your greatness, power, glory, victory, and majesty fills my existence. O LORD, Everything in the heavens and on earth is yours and I adore you as the one who is over all things." Amen. (1 Chronicles 29:11)*

Notes

Shoes for Chicken Little

For shoes, put on the peace that comes from the Good News, so that you will be fully prepared. (Ephesians 6:15)

An important part of every nursing uniform or attire is shoes. Shoes need to be comfortable, durable, and easy to clean. As Christians, our nursing shoes have an additional component. They are especially fitted with the gospel of peace, the message of Christ (Matthew 10:5-13). Jesus did not come to judge, nor cause war or conflict (John 12:47). Instead, he brought healing, peace, and forgiveness. This peaceful message is a special attribute of our nursing shoes (Acts 10:36).

One way we secure peace to our nursing shoes is by not allowing our minds and hearts to be absorbed by stress, anxiety, or fear. These emotions and responses come from our anxiety or from a spirit of fear, not the Holy Spirit (2 Timothy 1:7). Satan can capitalize on such emotions when looking for ways to distort our message or work.

I am reminded of a children's story/folk tale entitled *Chicken Little*[6]. It is about a chicken, who after having something fall on her head, runs in a panic yelling, "The sky is falling!" She runs to all her animal friends, Henny Penny, Turkey Lurkey, Goosey Loosey and others. Together they go to warn the king. Depending on the version, the animals either hide in a cave never warning the king, or they are able to warn the king, who then explains to Chicken Little and her friends about the large acorns falling from the trees.

Obviously, Chicken Little and her friends forgot their peaceful shoes and the promises of Christ (Philippians 4:7).

Read: Matthew 6:25-34

Reflect on how anxiety, stress, worry, and/or fear may have misdirected your life away from the peace of Christ.

Prayer: May the Lord of peace himself always give you his peace no matter what happens. Amen. (2 Thessalonians 3:16)

Notes

Looking for the One

> They worshiped together at the Temple each day, met in homes for the Lord's
> Supper, and shared their meals with great joy and generosity—all the while
> praising God and enjoying the goodwill of all people. (Acts 2:46-47)

When I was new nurse working in a hospital, I was shocked at the negativity that some of the nurses had towards their patients and their profession. I was excited to be a nurse and knew that the Lord had brought me through many personal trials in order to graduate and become an RN. There were very few Christians on the unit. I lacked fellow believers to guide and support me (Luke 8:4-8).

So, I prayed. I prayed against acquiring a bitter, complaining attitude (Ephesians 4:31). I prayed to keep a passion for nursing and the heart for patients that God had given me. Then one day, while reading a periodical, I saw an advertisement for a local Nurses Christian Fellowship (NCF) group in my area. I knew this was an answer to prayer. I immediately called the number and connected with other Christian nurses. This was over 23 years ago. Filling my need and answering my prayers, as well as the NCF groups' prayer, Jesus introduced me to NCF USA. I am now part of Nurses Christian Fellowship International and am connected to all of you—nurses who love Jesus and love nursing!

I tell this story to remind each of us that there are nurses everywhere who need fellowship and support to maintain their faith and passion for Christian nursing. They may feel discouraged and challenged to live out their love of Christ in their workplace. Jesus taught us to leave the 99 who are okay and seek out the one needing help (Matthew 18:12-14). We need to pray *and* actively seek out those out who need encouragement. Whether it is looking personally, locally, or nationally, seek out a sister or brother who needs YOU! Of course, if you are not connected to a fellowship of Christian nurses/healthcare providers, go to www.NCFI.org for more information.

Read: Matthew 18:12-14; Luke 8:4-8

Reflect on ways you can actively connect with other nurses to provide fellowship, prayer, and support.

Prayer: *Father, I thank you for connecting me to you. Help me connect with Christian nurses so that I may feast in fellowship with your supportive church. Amen.*

Notes

Revolutionary Nursing

Be happy about it! Be very glad! For a great reward awaits you in heaven. And remember, the ancient prophets were persecuted in the same way. (Matthew 5:12)

In the Sermon on the Mount (Matthew 5:3-12), Jesus gives an autobiography of his earthly life and he sets out the constitution of the Kingdom of God. He shows why Christians differ from non-Christians. This is not a law to be kept or imitated, but a new life to be lived. Jesus didn't give us an ethical code, but gave his life for us and shows us what a Christian life should be like. He gives us the Holy Spirit to enable us to experience a new life: Christ in us is the hope of glory (Colossians 1:27).

Nurses have to cope with caring for sick people who do not always appreciate the care they receive. Nurses have to cope with their own sorrows, grief, competition from colleagues, misunderstanding from patients and relatives, not to mention their own family problems. Nurses may have sacrificed everything for their patient's care and have no one to care for them. The teaching contained here, if accepted, gives us the strength to overcome disappointments, discrimination, rejection, and loneliness. Christian nurses are called by God to bring the presence of Jesus in nursing. Let us do this by living revolutionary lives, being completely satisfied for the glory of God.

Read: Matthew 5:3-12

Reflect on each teaching point in the Sermon on the Mount; choose one or two points to commit to revitalizing your nursing practice to be revolutionary like Jesus Christ.

Prayer: *Jesus, you called me to step beyond contemporary nursing to practice nursing in bold new ways. Amen.*

By Marion Deleen,
NCF Spain

Notes

Job Well Done!

> As we pray to our God and Father about you, we think of your faithful work, your loving deeds, and the enduring hope you have because of our Lord Jesus Christ. (1 Thessalonians 1:3)

These were the words of Apostle Paul to the believers in Thessalonica. Paul commended his Christian brothers and sisters for their faithfulness to the gospel message. Not only did Paul say, "Good job," to the believers, he also made a proclamation before God: "God as my witness, the Thessalonians are great Christians!" Paul recognized the believers' commitment to living out the teachings of Christ Jesus. They had faithfully served one another and Christ through acts of grace and charity (1 Thessalonians 4:9). In addition, their lives were an example to other Christians despite the persecution they endured (1:6-7, 2:14).

NCFI leaders, staff, fellow nurses and I want to express the same acclamation to you as Christian nurses committed to serving Jesus Christ. God knows of your work of faith in staying strong in Christ; your labour of love for patients and families, as well as for your fellow colleagues. NCFI commends your leadership and dedication to the national and regional fellowships. The work of these ministries builds up the body of Christ. NCFI also recognizes the steadfastness of your hope, developing from yesterday, providing strength for today, and guiding you in confidence for tomorrow.

The leaders and staff at NCFI remember you in their hearts and prayers, and proclaim to our God that you are a great Christian nurse. Job well done!

Read: 1 Thessalonians 1

Take time to say "Good job!" to a fellow nurse in person, via email, Twitter, or Facebook!

Prayer: *Father God, all of NCFI recognizes the great faithful work of Christian nurses worldwide, who depend on you to guide and encourage them for today and tomorrow! Amen.*

Notes

Faith to Rest

The disciples were absolutely terrified. "Who is this man?" they asked each other. "Even the wind and waves obey him!" (Mark 4:41)

A boat is traveling across the sea, when the wind and waves begin to toss the boat. Most of the people onboard are fearful. With each wave, the boat catches more and more water. One passenger is asleep on a cushion. The storm rages; the boat fills with water. Afraid they will be swallowed up by the sea, the passengers are in a panic, except for the lone passenger sleeping peacefully (Mark 4:35-41).

Our nursing boat is often rocked by storms. Our storms may be in the form of a change in funding, challenges to patient care, or not enough staff. We can quickly feel overwhelmed by the winds of change and find ourselves treading in the rising water of uncertainty. In fact, nursing and healthcare frequently experience some type of storm. The key to navigating our rocky nursing boat is in our response.

Do we frightfully pray to Jesus, "Don't you care that my unit is in shambles?" or "Why do we never have enough staff, supplies, etc.?" We may think we are resting assuredly on our healthcare ship, when in actuality we are not trusting. When we are busy bailing water or running in panic, it is hard to hear the Lord say, "Why are you afraid? Do you still have no faith?" (Mark 4:40).

Jesus rested in confidence on the storm-rocked boat; we can rest in him. Jesus cares about healthcare, nursing, and our patients. He will continue to guide and provide for you, me, and our patients. We may get a little wet from the splashing water, but we can trust in Jesus and rest in God's promises. God will calm the storm or he will calm us.

Read: Mark 4:35-41

What challenges or storms have rocked your healthcare boat? Do you sense Jesus rebuking you or providing words of assurance? What do you hear him saying to you during this stormy season?

Prayer: *Jesus, it is easy for me to worry about the challenges in healthcare, instead of trusting you. Help my faith, and set my heart and mind, to trust in you. Amen.*

Notes

Path to Humility

He was a devout, God-fearing man, as was everyone in his household. He gave generously to the poor and prayed regularly to God. (Acts 10:2)

The gentleman mentioned in the above Scripture is Cornelius (Acts 10). As a centurion, he was responsible for a legion of professional Roman soldiers numbering in the hundreds. He was a wealthy man of honor and position within the Roman government, his community, and his family. Regardless of his social and family status, all were aware that Cornelius was humble before God.

As a Roman citizen and warrior, Cornelius would not have considered himself as one of "God's chosen people." He approached God with a "sinner's heart," in need of mercy and undeserving of grace (Luke 18:13-14). Yahweh responded to his sincere heart and yearning spirit (Psalm 51:17). Cornelius, grateful for the acceptance and blessings of God, generously blessed others. From his wealth, Cornelius gave to the poor and provided for those around him. Cornelius' relationship with his servants, soldiers, and family was one of sincere service. The Lord honored this humble man by bringing the Good News through the Apostle Peter. Cornelius meekly accepted this miraculous event, submitting himself to God's will through a Jewish fisherman.

Like Cornelius, our path to humility begins by recognizing our true position before our most holy God. Bowed in gratefulness, we submit to God in reverence and lowliness of spirit (Matthew 5:3). Through a selfless spirit, we graciously give and serve our patients and colleagues, awed by the privilege we have been given. At the same time, we ensure pride, ego, and ambition are excised from our person (Philippians 2:1-11). True humility is an outward expression of an inward submissiveness to God, which reflects Christ our Lord.

Read: Philippians 2:1-11; Acts 10

Spend time in prayer reflecting on how you can embrace humility, personally and professionally.

Prayer: *O Lord, help me to love justice, live mercifully, and to walk humbly with you, reflecting your Son to all. Amen. (Micah 6:8)*

Notes

Spiritual Nutrition

[Jesus said] "People do not live by bread alone, but by every word that comes from the mouth of God." (Matthew 4:4)

When I reflect on the building blocks of nutrition for physical health, I am reminded of the importance of the building blocks for spiritual health. For example, in thinking of the protein found in fish, chicken, and beans that build muscle for physical strength, my thoughts turned to the building blocks of spiritual health. Just as malnourished patients lack healthy protein, we are spiritually malnourished without the living Messiah. Jesus is life; he provides the necessary strength for our spiritual foundation and life (John 1:3-4).

Starches, found in bread and rice, provide us with energy. In the same way, Scripture is our spiritual bread; it sustains our stamina throughout the day. We need to nourish our faith daily, through the reading and studying of God's Word (Deuteronomy 8:3; Matthew 6:11).

Vegetables supply the nutrients for each cell in our bodies. Many of us have diets that lack an adequate intake of vegetables. Similarly, I couldn't help but compare prayer to our intake of vegetables. Although prayer is vital for our faith, we seem to fall short on our servings, i.e., amount of time and thought we spend in prayer (Luke 5:16; 1 Thessalonians 5:17).

Another nutrient important to our faith is found in praise and worship. I think of this as fruit. When we lift our voices in song, exalting the goodness and excellence of our gracious Heavenly Father, we experience the sweetness of his presence. This sweetness is rich in nutrients, and we can hunger for more and more! (Hebrews 13:15)

Not unlike our physical body, which requires a balanced diet, our spirit needs a steady diet of essential nutrients. Eat from the bounty of the Lord's table, feasting on all the sustenance he provides, both physically and spiritually (Psalm 23:5; Matthew 22:1-2).

Read: Individual verses quoted above.

Reflect on your spiritual diet? Is there an essential component or two missing? What changes can you make to feast on all the Lord has provided?

Prayer: *Father God, thank you for all the sustenance you have blessed me with. May I come to your table more often and feast in your presence. Amen.*

Notes

A Banner of Thankfulness

Always be joyful. Never stop praying. Be thankful in all circumstances, for this is
God's will for you who belong to Christ Jesus. (1 Thessalonians 5:16-18)

One of the true marks of maturity for a Christian is the ability to be thankful
in all circumstances. This isn't a meaningless chant. Being thankful in all
circumstances is truly finding something for which to thank God. This
thankfulness is seen in a terminally ill child thanking God for loving parents; a
woman who has been abused thanking Jesus for her children; a person with
schizophrenia thanking God for modern medications; a death-row prisoner
thanking God for a fellow brother or sister in the Lord. These are examples of
people expressing gratitude to God (1 Peter 1:6; Romans 5:1-5).

One way to spur a personal attitude of gratefulness is to recognize God for
each and every providence. The writer of Psalm 136 narrates an excellent
template for recognizing God's intercessory hand in our lives. The psalmist starts
by calling all to, "Give thanks to the Lord," and then he lists various reasons why
the reader should be thankful: "[God] is good…, God of gods…, does great
wonders…, made the heavens…" (vs. 1-9). Depending on the translation, a
repetitive refrain concludes each stanza with God's "steadfast love endures
forever" or "loving kindness endures forever." This refrain declares the heavenly
Father's covenant, compassionate care for his children, as part of an intimate
relationship

The psalmist continues with a history lesson of how the Lord intervened in
the lives of the Israelites. The Lord's intercessory hand demonstrated his
covenant relationship with the Israelites by parting the Red Sea and remembering
their weaknesses (vs. 13, 23).

This Lord is our Lord. He wrote, and continues to write, our personal
historical narrative. When we struggle to find something to be thankful for, we
can pause and thank the Creator. He has provided for our existence the
necessities of air and water for life. Through a brief history lesson we can offer
thanks for the continued hope that strengthens our faith.

Read: Psalm 136

Fill in the following blank: "Give thanks to the Lord for _____."
Describe how the Lord has demonstrated his "steadfast love" for you personally.

Prayer: *O Lord, I praise your name which means: "compassionate and gracious, slow to anger,
abounding in love and faithfulness." Amen. (Psalm 86:15)*

Notes

Critical Reminders

[Jesus said] "But when the Father sends the Advocate as my representative—that is, the Holy Spirit—he will teach you everything and will remind you of everything I have told you." (John 14:26)

As a nursing instructor, I provide my students critical reminders for safe patient care in the hospital. For example: "Wash your hands," "Put the side-rails up," "Verify the patient's name," and other important prompts. As the students advance to their next nursing courses, I hope they will remember these essential points. I am reaffirmed in my teaching when they approach me in the hall and say, "Carrie, when I was with a patient this week, I remembered what you said. It was like your voice was in my head, reminding me of those critical points from my first semester." We laugh as I enjoy our discussion. In the back of my mind, I am hoping the voice they hear is my "good voice" and not the "crazy teacher" voice.

These experiences remind me of Jesus' final lecture to his disciples in John 14—17. He was about to leave and knew it was imperative to provide his critical reminders: "I am in the Father and the Father is in me" (14:10-11); "Remain in me and I will remain in you" (15:1-4); "I have loved you even as the Father has loved me. Remain in my love" (15:9) and others.

In addition to his critical points, Jesus knew the disciples would need personal assistance. As they faced persecution and endured trials, the disciples needed supernatural help, so, Jesus provided the disciples with a Counselor or Advisor—the Holy Spirit (14:15-17). All of Jesus' teachings, his exemplary living, and his insight into God the Father are embodied in the Holy Spirit. The Helper is eternal and continues to communicate spiritual wisdom and growing knowledge of vital truth to all Christians. We have the New Testament as our critical reminders, and through the indwelling of the Holy Spirit, Jesus ensured his continued presence throughout eternity (John 14:18-20).

Read: John 14:16-18, 26, 15:26, 16:5-15

Think back to some critical reminders you have received from the Holy Spirit. How have they influenced your personal faith and/or nursing care?

Prayer: *Thank you Jesus, for the promised Holy Spirit in our lives, communicating your teachings to us. Amen.*

Notes

Unspoken Prayers

The smoke of the incense, mixed with the prayers of God's holy people, ascended up to God from the altar where the angel had poured them out. (Revelation 8:4)

The clinic on the edge of the village reaches out to the underserved. With very little staffing, the nurse completes the intake forms, assesses symptoms, and provides education, while listening to a new mom concerned about her malnourished toddler. A young teenager is seen for abuse. A husband is treated for a chronic disease, in hopes he will still be able to provide for his family. Later, to benefit the most patients, the nurse rations out the limited supply of medications.

The day is long, and the sun sets as the nurse rides the dilapidated bus through the crime-ridden city to home. Disquiet permeates the night. The bus riders are anxious about personal safety and/or coping with grief. Some are disgruntled, others neglected. The nurse's thoughts flit from tight finances, preparations for the flu season, and contemplation on the needs of the clinic's patients.

Once home, the nurse wearily prepares dinner, helps with homework, and coordinates the following day's schedule. Finally, with the moon high in the star-bright sky, the nurse stops and sighs, "O Lord, where do I begin?" Before the prayer ascends to heaven, the Lord responds, "I am here, my devoted child." Unbeknownst to the nurse, the Lord has delivered, protected, answered, and rescued throughout the seemingly endless day. His answers have quietly cared for patients, opened the hearts of those with money, and brought wisdom to the nurse's mind.

Our spoken and unspoken prayers ascend to the throne of God where, unassumingly the Holy Spirit intercedes in our lives, working out the Lord's will for both us and our patients (Romans 8:27). Praise the Lord for his miraculous, discreet care.

Read: Matthew 7:7-11

Review a recent work day. Where can you sense that the Lord intervened to answer your unspoken prayers?

Prayer: *Lord, help me to trust in the Holy Spirit's intercessions in my work as a nurse, and open my eyes to the hidden answers to my prayers. Amen.*

Notes

Secured in Faithfulness

> He will cover you with his feathers. He will shelter you with his wings. His faithful promises are your armor and protection. (Psalm 91:4)

Have you ever seen an adult bird tuck a baby bird under its wings? The adult bird has the advantage of being larger and more mature. It has acquired life-learning wisdom and is alert to the surrounding dangers. The baby chick rests securely, tucked closely for warmth and comfort. It is weak and vulnerable, dependent upon its parent for sustenance. The hatchling has no knowledge of anything beyond the warmth and safety of the parent. This is true security.

Through the simple, intimate life of a bird, we are taught about God's protection—his faithfulness. Some Bibles translate *truth* to mean stability, firmness, and reliability. At first we may be confused by the use of word *truth* in relation to *faithfulness*. Actually, the Lord's truth is the basis for our strength and security. The divine teachings of the Bible, and the authenticity of Jesus Christ, are truth, and an expression of the faithfulness of God.

Romans 3:3-4 reminds us of the indescribable law at work with God's faithfulness—it isn't dependent upon us as believers. Whether we believe in it or not, God's faithfulness does not change. As children of the Creator, our challenge is to be like the baby bird, resting securely under our Father's wings. Are we secure and content, trusting our Protector's faithfulness? Or are we panicking, constantly peeking between the feathers to make sure all is okay? The choice is ours.

Read: Psalm 91

As you read through Psalm 91, reflect on the various ways the Lord intervenes for you. (e.g. rescue, etc.).

Prayer: *Father God, help me not to peek nor panic as your faithfulness secures my life under the covering of your wings. Amen*

Notes

24/7 Protection

Do not be afraid of the terrors of the night, nor the arrow that flies in the day. Do not dread the disease that stalks in darkness, nor the disaster that strikes at midday. (Psalm 91:5-6)

What is your greatest fear? Is it your loved one experiencing illness and suffering? Is it the threat of living with unrelieved pain or a terminal diagnosis? What about the unknown of aging: does the prospect of disability, confusion, or dementia frighten you? Do you dread the torture or violence of wickedness encroaching into your community? Maybe your anxiety or distress is more along the lines of staying faithful. Perhaps you fear denouncing Christ if persecuted, or falling into sin, or being overwhelmed by evil? These examples are enough to send even the most devout running fearfully for protection.

In the previous reflection in Psalm 91, we explored God's faithfulness. This powerful psalm also reminds us of the extent of the Lord's protective hand. At first read, we may assume nothing bad will happen to us. That, however, is not the purpose of the psalm, nor is it true. We live in an evil world with disease, tragedy, and death. Our confidence does not rest in nothing happening to us or our families. Instead, we are assured that nothing is beyond the reach of God (Psalm 139:7-12). No sin or evil will prevent the faithful hand of our Lord from guiding us. There may come a time in each of our lives when we quake in fear, run in panic, and hide in terror. The Most High and Almighty will be with us there. We have a 24/7 security system, with the Lord ensuring international and eternal coverage. This coverage is mediated and delivered through the promises of our glorious Saviour, ensuring that even death should not cause us to worry (1 Corinthians 15:26, 55; Romans 6:8).

Read: Romans 8:31-39

What causes you the most fear? How can the passage in Romans be an antidote for your personal fear(s)?

Prayer: *Father God, help me to rest in your 24/7 eternal protection, ensuring I will someday dwell with you and your Son. Amen.*

Notes

Choose Joy

[Jesus said] "I have told you these things so that you will be filled with my joy. Yes, your joy will overflow!" (John 15:11).

It was a typical day in a medical unit of a hospital. One of my patients was an older adult in her 70s, with a history of diabetes and bilateral amputation of her legs, secondary to peripheral vascular disease. She had been admitted during the night with pneumonia and was doing well with antibiotics and oxygen. As I entered her room, a boisterous voice called to me, "Good morning! Are you my nurse today?"

I stopped in my tracks, not quite sure what to think. "Yes, I am. I am Carrie. You sound like you are doing well."

"I am doing wonderful," she exclaimed, moving herself independently from the hospital bed to her wheel chair.

"Here, let me help you," I said while putting my stuff down and rushing to her side.

"No, no. I am fine," she said, brushing me off. "I do this all the time." As she repositioned herself, she casually replied. "I may not have legs, but that hasn't stopped me from getting around."

At first, I was surprised by her bold statement. As the day went by, I noticed how well she moved and cared for herself. Her independence was impressive, yet, most amazing was her joyful attitude, which never swayed. Later in the afternoon, she shared how since she had lost her second leg, she had chosen joy. She had been adamant in refusing to allow despair and depression to rule her life.

Later, as I reflected on my patient's attitude, I realized she could have been angry or fearful. She could have been demanding and expecting sympathy or special services related to her circumstances. Instead, she had embraced the "joy of the Lord." She had chosen to live life to the fullest—minus a couple of body parts.

Read: Philippians 1:3-30

Reflect on this definition of joy[7]: "Christian joy is no mere gaiety that knows no gloom, but is the result of the triumph of faith over adverse and trying circumstances, which, instead of hindering, actually enhance it."

Prayer: *Jesus, the joy you give is not measured through circumstances, nor in comparison with the world's happiness. Help me look beyond my human experiences to find you—Joy! Amen.*

Notes

NG

The harvesters are paid good wages, and the fruit they harvest is people brought
to eternal life. What joy awaits both the planter and the harvester alike! You know
the saying, 'One plants and another harvests.' And it's true. (John 4:36-37)

One of the exciting things about nursing is seeing the students and young
nurses entering our profession. They burst into the hospitals, clinics, and facilities
with fresh energy and innovations. This is especially true for the next generation
(NG) of Christian nurses. They not only love Jesus and are passionate about
serving him, they are dedicated to empowering one another for excellence. With
the heart of an older sibling and a seasoned professional, I want to encourage
these young nurses. They are the future of nursing. Using 2 Timothy, here is a
personal blessing to the NG nurses:

*I spiritually lay my hands on you and anoint your work in nursing as holy. I encourage
you to nurture your spiritual gifts through prayer and discernment, while holding onto to the wise
teachings you have received (2 Timothy 1:6, 3:14-17). Take time to fuse your nursing
knowledge with the faith and love found in our Lord, Jesus Christ. Through the strength of the
Holy Spirit, guard the gospel entrusted to you, staying clear of ministry disputes or fruitless
arguments (1:13, 2:23-24). As challenges come along, stay committed to the plans the Lord has
for you. Depend upon Jesus' faithfulness to sustain you, both personally and professionally.
Amen.*

As older siblings in Christ, we commit to the following support: We will pray
for you and the work of the Holy Spirit. We will endeavor to unite us as one body
(3:17). We gladly share our expertise and knowledge to build up the body of
Christ and the nursing profession (3:10). We also pledge to live exemplary lives,
full of purpose and endurance. Lastly, we will be persistent in faith and good
works that produces an abundant harvest. A harvest that is ready to be reaped by
you, our NG of nurses (John 4:38).

Read: 2 Timothy 2

To both NG nurses and older siblings: find new ways to reach across generations
and connect for a bountiful eternal harvest.

Prayer: *Father God, since you are the master Harvester, guide us in collaborating together so we
can be effective labourers in your Kingdom, producing abundant crops that fill the cisterns of
heaven! Amen*

Notes

But, Lord!?

"But Lord," exclaimed Ananias, "I've heard about the terrible things this man has done to the believers in Jerusalem!"(Acts 9:13)

Many may know the story of the Apostle Paul, who was previously called Saul. Ananias a "disciple of the Lord" was instrumental in Paul's conversion to Christianity. The Lord came to Ananias in a vision, directing him to go and present the gospel to Saul. Previously, Saul had violently persecuted Christians. So when Ananias received this personal directive from God, he argued essentially saying, "Excuse me, Lord, do you know who this Paul is?" Ananias trembled with fear. He was unsure if the Lord was really saying, "Go to Saul."

Fear is a powerful deterrent in our obedience to God. Most of us will probably not be directed by God to talk with someone frightening or to go someplace fearful. On the other hand, we may be directed to take on an unfamiliar role in nursing or provide care for patients different from ourselves. It is almost assured that God will, at some point, ask us to do or say something that is troublesome or uncomfortable (Matthew 10:26-31).

The Lord responded to Ananias' fear by saying, "Go, because this man (Saul) is my chosen instrument to carry my name before Gentiles and kings and the people of Israel" (Acts 9:15). Hence, Ananias followed the Lord's instructions and met with Saul, baptizing him. Saul received love and forgiveness through Ananias.

The Lord will call on us and we will be frightened. We may even be tempted to respond, "But, Lord?" Depend on the Lord to guide, strengthen, and most importantly, work through you for his glory.

Read: Acts 9:1-19

Has there been a time when fear, insecurity, or doubt prevented you from obeying God's directive?

Prayer: *Jesus, I come to you with an obedient heart, committed to doing your will. Help me overcome my fears and give me resolve to live out your directives. Amen*

Notes

Who Am I?

Sin is crouching at the door, eager to control you. But you must subdue it and be its master. (Genesis 4:7)

See if you can identify the following human attribute…I am a vector-borne parasite that is transmitted from one host to another. Like a pathogen, once I gain access to the human host, a simple deceitful thought or idea blights the mind. Any logical knowledge and intelligible reasoning that is in contrast to me is distorted. Once infected, my victims only think and gain knowledge contributing to my reproduction.

I also invade the soft, tender heart, removing kind and gracious attitudes toward others, especially those of different social, economic, religious, or ethnic groups. This putrid, infected, contaminated heart vivaciously spreads venom, even assaulting innocent children. As a multiple organ systemic pathogen, I especially feast on the soul or spirit. Here, I relish in doing the most damage. For in the soul, inner thoughts, exterior actions, and cherished relationships develop. With the soul contaminated, I oust the indwelling Spirit, preventing mercy and love from diluting my growing loath and rank. In time, I will invade and gain control of all organs. Gradually, I direct the eyes to focus, the ears to listen, and the mouth to spew forth further acts of abomination and animosity.

Once I have successfully conquered the host, I easily spread to spouses, children, and relatives. Like a pandemic, my outbreak will contaminate neighbors and friends, communities and nations. Unaware to the original host, I am in complete control of the human and will reside until death. Who am I?

I am hate—a simple, four-letter word that wreaks havoc on individuals, groups, communities, and societies. Even a little bit of malice wounds each individual, as well as others.

The only cure to hatred is love. The selfless action of God's love is the only enemy of hate—not knowledge, not money, nor spiritual enlightenment. Love is a chemotherapy of sorts that can remove hate and bring all those infected within the beautiful mercy of Christ.

Read: Proverbs 6:16-19; 1 John 3 & 4

Contrast the seven human characteristics the Lord hates with the love of God discussed in 1 John.

Prayer: *Father God, it is so easy to get sucked into insidious attitudes that are hateful. Cleanse and guide me into living a life purified by your love. Amen.*

Notes

Seed of Influence

Jesus said, "[The kingdom of God] is like a tiny mustard seed that a man planted in a garden; it grows and becomes a tree, and the birds make nests in its branches." (Luke 13:19)

Most nurses entering the nursing profession do not say, "I want to be a nurse manager or charge nurse?" Instead, nurses enter the profession to care for patients. Even when the opportunity for advancement is presented, many times, nurses refuse. They seemingly run away from anything that looks like administrative or managerial duties. Many nurses don't want to trade patient care for employee evaluations, budget meetings, and strategic plans. This seems to be even more common among Christian nurses. For with a servant's heart, their only desire is to care for their patients. On the other hand, leadership positions are a great way for Christian nurses to impact those within units, hospitals, schools, and institutions.

As managers and administrators, nurses can be the presence of Christ beyond their interactions with individual patients and staff. Nurses can create policies that reflect Christian excellence in patient care. The wisdom of biblical stewardship can be integrated into budget meetings. As a supportive, compassionate manager, staff evaluations can reflect the heart of Christ. Leadership is not necessarily a place of power, nor does it distance nurses from the favored place of patient care. It is a position of influence for quality performance.

Comparable to planting small seeds, Christian nurses can cultivate their staff into fruit bearing trees. As nurses step-up to leadership positions, the Holy Spirit works through them to produce caring environments within hospitals, clinics and colleges, and this contributes to the transformation of the healthcare systems. Much is accomplished through the planting of individual seeds.

Read: 2 Corinthians 9:6-13

Have you hesitated to move into a leadership role? If so, discuss your concerns. On the other hand, if you are currently in a leadership role, reflect on how your influence represents Christ in your work place.

Prayer: *Holy Spirit, open my heart to how I can influence those within my unit, clinic, or institution as a nursing leader. Amen.*

Notes

A Powerful Encounter

"Who do you say I am?" Simon Peter answered, "You are the Messiah, the Son of the living God." (Matthew 16:15-16)

With burning hatred, Saul traveled to Damascus seeking to imprison and destroy the radical disciples of the Way. During his journey, God miraculously intervened and blinded Saul, while interrogating him with, "Why are you persecuting me!" Dazed and confused, Saul spent three days in holy darkness, stunned by his encounter with the Christ (Acts 9:1-9).

Biblical scholars are confident that Saul had met Jesus before. Even though Scripture does not tell us, Saul was probably well-acquainted with the labeled "trouble maker" called Jesus. It is also quite possible Saul had witnessed Jesus perform miracles and had heard his teachings. Nonetheless, Saul's heart had remained resistant to this so-called Messiah, rejecting Jesus' claim as Israel's fulfilled hope. It took a drastic, post-resurrection encounter with the *all powerful* (Revelation 1:8), to expose Saul's heart to the true identity of Israel's Savior. The result was not only Saul's salvation, but a new man emerged. Saul, now Paul, was a transformed disciple, instrumental in bringing the Gospel to the Gentiles scattered throughout the Roman Empire.

We all have family, friends, and even colleagues who have closed their hearts to the true identity of Jesus. Like Saul, they may know Jesus, but are blind to the grace and love found in the Savior (2 Corinthians 4:4). Let's stay steadfast in prayer and love for those who need a powerful encounter with the living Christ. Let's pray that they will see beyond the man or the myth, in order to experience the true Messiah.

Read: Matthew 16:13-19; Acts 9:1-9

Spend time specifically praying for friends, family members, and colleagues who need a powerful encounter with Jesus!

Prayer: *I praise and thank you, Jesus for revealing yourself to me. Help me to proclaim your truth to others through both word and deed. Amen.*

Notes

In the Trenches

> Remember that Christians all over the world are going through the same kind of suffering you are. (1 Peter 5:9)

I am unsure how many people are familiar with the expression or metaphor "in the trenches." It is a reference from World War I when front-line soldiers lived and fought in deep ditches or trenches. These were the men who crossed the fields to battle one-on-one with the enemy. They were dirty and bloody, malnourished, wounded and sick; yet their bravery and determination was a successful tactic for the war.

This same reference can be applied to Christians around the world who wage war against spiritual forces of darkness: "For we are not fighting against people made of flesh and blood, but against the evil rulers and authorities of the unseen world, against those mighty powers of darkness who rule this world, and against wicked spirits in the heavenly realms" (Ephesians 6:12).

All Christians are soldiers in a spiritual war. At times, the fight feels like trench warfare, with individual scrimmages and tactical maneuvers. Some of us may feel bloody and dirty from the hand-to-hand combat. Maybe some are in the infirmary being patched back together by our pastors, Bible study leaders, and prayer warriors. And I am sure, many Christians are exhausted and malnourished, feeling alone in the trenches, looking for reinforcements.

Next time you feel spiritually bruised and tattered, hold fast for you are not alone. Across the border, beyond the continent, and around the globe, millions of our brothers and sisters fight the same war. We are in the trenches standing firm together in victory through the unity of the Holy Spirit (Ephesians 4:4).

Read: 2 Corinthians 11:23-33

How are you encouraged by knowing Christians around the world are also persevering for Christ? Make a plan to pray for our fellow comrades around the world.

Prayer: *Father God, thank you for the reminder that I am not alone in the trenches. Remind me to pray for my comrades who are also battle weary. Amen.*

Notes

Missteps for Opportunity

> Great is his [God's] faithfulness; his mercies begin afresh each morning.
> (Lamentations 3:23)

A nursing student receives an unsatisfactory grade in a nursing course. Heart broken, he is unable to continue the program. A new graduate fails the licensing exam in nursing. Devastated, she is forced to hold off her plans to start a new job. Another nurse is overwhelmed and stressed at the demands and skills required for a busy trauma unit, and is let-go from his dream position. He returns to the job market, dejected and disappointed.

Each example reminds us that there is the potential for failure in nursing. Yet, failures or missteps are opportunities for personal growth and transformational faith. For through these experiences we see the Lord's hand and wisdom, guiding us to previously unseen doors (Proverbs 16:9).

Let's take the above examples and add potential opportunities:

The nursing student who is unable to complete the current program applies to a different program. Here the student connects with a nursing colleague that mentors and assists the student, fulfilling his dream to become a missionary nurse to underserved countries. The graduate who failed the licensing exam, takes the exam again and is successful, thus learning a valuable lesson in perseverance, humility, and wisdom that serves her well as she attends graduate school for a degree in nursing education. The nurse who couldn't keep up with the demands of a trauma unit, discovers his real dream of a serving as a Family Nurse Practitioner. In this setting, he can demonstrate patience, compassion, and communication to provide excellent nursing care to diverse families.

Many times we want to focus on our failures, when these missteps can be opportunities to grow and be used by God in unique ways. Next time you are stumbling on your nursing journey, look for where the Father's hand is transforming you into a new person (2 Corinthians 5:17).

Read: Acts 28:11-31

The above reading is on Paul's life as a prisoner in Rome. How might have Paul's perceptions been as a "prisoner" compared to God's plan for success as a writer/preacher under house arrest?

Prayer: *Father, we see failures and missteps in our lives as negative, where you see opportunities to work out Your will in our lives. Give us faith to see You amidst all our steps. Amen*

Notes

References

Ashworth, P.M.(2012). *A History of Nurses Christian Fellowship International: The First 50 years*. Blackstaff Press, Belfast. p. xv

1. Dictionaries: *Hope*. Retrieved from: https://www.blueletterbible.org/search/Dictionary/viewTopic.cfm?topic=IT0004415. International Standard Bible Encyclopedia

2. Dameron, C.M. (2007). Ready, Set, Rest? *Journal of Christian Nursing*, 24(4), 194-198. doi:10.1097/01.CNJ.0000291533.48435.4d

3. Greek Lexicon: splagchnizomai G4697 (KJV). Retrieved from: http://www.blueletterbible.org/lang/lexicon/lexicon.cfm?Strongs=G4697&t=KJV

4. Hebrew Lexicon: *Koach* H3581 (KJV). Retrieved from: https://www.blueletterbible.org/lang/lexicon/lexicon.cfm?Strongs=H3581&t=KJV

5. Dameron, C.M. (2013) Excellence *Our Faithful Journey in Nursing*. Kindle book. http://www.amazon.com/Faithful-Journey-Nursing-Carrie-Dameron-ebook/dp/B00E1T4VIS

6. Chicken Little: https://en.wikipedia.org/wiki/Henny_Penny

7. Dictionaries: *Joy*. Retrieved from: https://www.blueletterbible.org/search/Dictionary/viewTopic.cfm?topic=IT0005175. International Standard Bible Encyclopedia.

Resources

NCFI (Nurses Christian Fellowship International) reaches around the world connecting nurses through local groups, national fellowships and global regions. Visit their website for more information on how you can become connected with NCFI in your country!

Website: www.ncfi.org

Follow NCFI on Facebook: https://www.facebook.com/visit.ncfi/

NG Next Generation: is the international student nurse group dedicated to reaching out and encouraging merging professionals. Visit their Facebook page and sign up for their monthly "pray around the world." https://www.facebook.com/ncfi.ng

NCFI Cares: a bimonthly devotion for international nurses. Subscribe to receive via email at: http://ncfi.org/resources/ncfi-cares-devotionals/

Journal of Christian Nursing is a peer-reviewed, quarterly, professional print and online publication of Nurses Christian Fellowship, USA. The journal helps students, nurses, and educators practice from a biblically-based, Christian perspective. International nurses can have online access at $37/year! An amazing offer! Visit http://ncf-jcn.org/resources/international-online-access

Christian Nursing 101 a column discussing the tenents of Christian faith while exploring applicable skills to the nursing profession.

Our Faithful Journey in Nursing by Carrie M. Dameron (2013), is a teaching on four essential concepts for Christian nursing: faith, compassion, prayer and excellence. Each concept is explored using both biblical and nursing experts to support the discussion. Supplemental biblical based study questions encourage the reader to examine and apply each concept to their nursing practice. The study questions are written for both individual and group study. Available e-book: http://www.amazon.com/Faithful-Journey-Nursing-Carrie-Dameron-ebook/dp/B00E1T4VIS

About the Author

If you read the preface, then you know that I gave my life to Christ as an adult. I was raised Mormon amidst a chaotic and troubled home life. I faced many personal difficulties as a young girl, an emotional mess of adolescence, and a rough start to adulthood. As I struggled to deal with my painful childhood, raise my two daughters, and navigate a troubled marriage, I began searching for something to heal my past, bring significance to my life, and guide my future. I explored various spiritual philosophies and religious claims. While working at a restaurant and taking prerequisites for nursing, a bar tender invited me to a Christian church. As a Mormon, I had always known God, but didn't know about Jesus.

Fast-forward two years. One day in February, as I sat in the pastor's office (who happened to be an ex-Mormon), the pastor told me about this beautiful gift that God gives us—his Son. I imagined a large box wrapped with beautiful, colorful paper decorated with an enormous bow. I didn't need to do anything but accept and open the gift. I opened this amazing gift—and found my redeemer Jesus, the living Christ. To say it radically transformed my life, is an understatement. Jesus rocked my world and life has never been the same.

I faced challenging times as a new Christian, *but* Jesus kept me on the right path, healed my past, and guided my future. I am a living testimony of Jesus' complete healing, enduring strength, and guiding grace. My life verse or parable is Luke 5:24-25 where Jesus heals the paralytic, "And at once he rose up before them and took up the mat he had been lying on and went home, glorifying God." Like this man, Jesus gave me a new life and guided me in learning to walk differently, while leaving the pain of my past behind (my mat). I became a nurse…and now I teach nursing at the same school where I met Jesus☺!

Twenty-six years later, the Lord has remained faithful to his promises and directs my path. My prayer is to spend my life glorifying God through the joy and grace he continues to give me.

When I am not teaching, nor writing I am enjoying trail running, hiking, and 5 grandchildren!

Education & Experience

I am Associate Professor of Nursing at Ohlone College in California, USA where I teach two-year nursing students. I have a Masters in Nursing, with emphasis on administration/education; Advanced Certification in adult medical/surgical nursing. My experience includes 24 years in adult/elder acute care, 5 years in hospice/home care, and 14 years in academics.

Final Note

I am excited to have partnered with Nurses Christian Fellowship International (NCFI) for **CARES**. If you have been encouraged by the reflections, then consider making a donation to NCFI at www.ncfi.org

Send me a "hi" or "like" or "comment"

http://blog.carriedameron.com/
https://www.facebook.com/CarrieMDameron/
www.carriedameron.com
@CarrieDameron

www.ingramcontent.com/pod-product-compliance
Lightning Source LLC
Chambersburg PA
CBHW060524030426

42337CB00015B/1989